6.99

 University of
Chester

This book is to be returned on or before the last date stamped below. Overdue charges will be incurred by the late return of books.

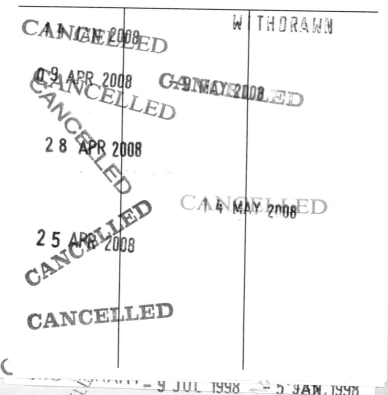

The Critics Debate

General Editor Michael Scott

Published titles

Sons and Lovers Geoffrey Harvey
Bleak House Jeremy Hawthorn
The Canterbury Tales Alcuin Blamires
Tess of the d'Urbervilles Terence Wright
The Waste Land and Ash Wednesday Arnold P. Hinchliffe
Paradise Lost Margarita Stocker
King Lear Ann Thompson
Othello Peter Davison
The Winter's Tale Bill Overton
Gulliver's Travels Brian Tippett
Blake: Songs of Innocence and Experience David Lindsay
Measure for Measure T.F. Wharton
Hamlet Michael Hattaway
The Tempest David Daniell
Coriolanus Bruce King
Wuthering Heights Peter Miles
The Metaphysical Poets Donald Mackenzie
The Great Gatsby Stephen Matterson
Heart of Darkness Robert Burden
To the Lighthouse Su Reid
Portrait of a Lady/Turn of the Screw David Kirby
Hard Times Allen Samuels
Philip Larkin Stephen Regan

Further titles are in preparation

HARD TIMES

An Introduction to the
Variety of Criticism

Allen Samuels

M
MACMILLAN

For my parents

First published 1992 by
MACMILLAN EDUCATION LTD
Houndmills, Basingstoke, Hampshire RG21 2XS
and London
Companies and representatives
throughout the world

ISBN 0–333–45933–4 hardcover
ISBN 0–333–45934–2 paperback

A catalogue record for this book is available
from the British Library.

Typeset by Footnote Graphics,
Warminster, Wiltshire
Printed in Hong Kong

Contents

6   CONTENTS

General Editor's Preface

Over the last few years the practice of literary criticism has become hotly debated. Methods developed earlier in the century and before have been attacked and the word 'crisis' has been drawn upon to describe the present condition of English Studies. That such a debate is taking place is a sign of the subject discipline's health. Some would hold that the situation necessitates a radical alternative approach which naturally implies a 'crisis situation'. Others would respond that to employ such terms is to precipitate or construct a false position. The debate continues but it is not the first. 'New Criticism' acquired its title because it attempted something fresh, calling into question certain practices of the past. Yet the practices it attacked were not entirely lost or negated by the new critics. One factor becomes clear: English Studies is a pluralistic discipline.

What are students coming to advanced work in English for the first time to make of all this debate and controversy? They are in danger of being overwhelmed by the cross-currents of critical approaches as they take up their study of literature. The purpose of this series is to help delineate various critical approaches to specific literary texts. Its authors are from a variety of critical schools and have approached their task in a flexible manner. Their aim is to help the reader come to terms with the variety of criticism and to introduce him or her to further reading on the subject and to a fuller evaluation of a particular text by illustrating the way it has been approached in a number of contexts. In the first part of the book a critical survey is given of some of the major ways the text has been appraised. This is done sometimes in a thematic manner, sometimes according to various 'schools' or 'approaches'. In the second part the authors provide their own appraisals of the text from their stated critical standpoint, allowing the reader the knowledge of their own particular approaches from which their views may in turn be evaluated. The series therein hopes to introduce and to elucidate criticism of authors and texts being studied and to encourage participation as the critics debate.

Michael Scott

A Note on Text and References

All references to *Hard Times* are to the Penguin edition, edited by David Craig (Harmondsworth, 1969), and are given in square brackets. References to secondary material appear in parentheses with date of publication on the introduction of each such work. Fuller details may then be found in the bibliography where secondary works are listed in alphabetical order.

Acknowledgements

My thanks are due to Alcuin Blamires and Elsie Reynolds for early encouragement, and to Peter Miles who, as ever, acted above and beyond the call of duty that one can reasonably expect from a busy colleague. I must also thank Monica Norden who produced the typescript from my execrable handwriting. Her calm patience was matched only by that of Mike Scott and of the editorial staff at Macmillan who treated this errant author so sympathetically.

Allen Samuels

Introduction

Introduction

'The difficulty of the space is CRUSHING', wrote Charles Dickens to his friend and eventual biographer, John Forster, as he wrestled with *Hard Times*, the ninth of his major novels, and the shortest. For a writer used to writing for monthly serial publication, and not for weekly instalments, as here, and for whom the relative brevity of 117,000 words is to be measured against the 350,000 words of *Bleak House* or *David Copperfield* it is hardly surprising he could jokingly complain that his 'perpetual rushing at the work [made him] three parts mad and the fourth delirious.' Similar anxieties are promised to anyone attempting to deal with even a fraction of the vast critical debate which has accumulated around this least liked of Dickens's works. Inevitably, some critics will be lost in the crush as the variety of critical approach is temporarily subdued to a semblance of manageable proportions. In a short study such as this semblance is the operative work.

Roland Barthes observed somewhere that 'what is significant is what gets signified.' This is not merely a tautology dressed up in the Gallic fondness for aphorism and paradox. Significance carries within it its meanings of 'important', 'worth talking about', 'valued'. It is thus a useful reminder that what is highlighted, given prominence, praised, even made available for discussion in comparison to what is marginalised, denigrated, or even omitted altogether, is as much a function of the critics, and the times in which they write, as of the texts they read.

Critics are, after all, writers too. Within the recent history of critical writing it might appear that critics are more interested in their reading of the text than the text itself; the latter is but an occasion for the act of writing. But all critics of whatever disposition, even the least humble and most egocentric, have to accept the disciplining proposition that novels are not written to the (often imaginary) logical, methodical, theoretical set of ideas which critics impose upon them. Criticism has its procedures, and fiction has its procedures, and the distance between them is what ensures the critical function to continue. Some critics, it is true, have shown a certain resistance to according texts a primary status, and wish to substitute their own singular and idiosyncratic versions of what the text means by re-writing it in ways for their own purposes, re-writings supported by an ever-increasing, ever-elaborate apparatus of theory.

Anthropologically-minded critics, for instance, can call this re-writing the killing of the father, and Freudian-minded critics talk of anxious resistance to precursor poets, and ideology-hunting critics talk of finding the hidden within the text and feminists discuss the phallocentric. These approaches are dramatising and sometimes bleakly dehumanising analogies, or metaphors, for the selective critical processes any critic engages in discussing a text. Whatever their emphasis, and they do differ violently, they inevitably make literary criticism self-conscious, and they thus prompt us to ask why we, or indeed any writer, should have taken the line he/she did. The different standpoints acknowledge criticism as a variant reading extended to its final limit of writing.

A history of the continuing debate of criticism is no different; it too is what gets noticed at any one time because this is what the critics have chosen to signify at that moment in history out of all the possible interpretations of texts. In reality, the total critical debate is in potential everything which has ever been said about every aspect of *Hard Times*, a prospect which is as dismally uninviting as it is, thankfully, unrealisable. A history of critical debate is no different from all histories; it is fabricated out of the raw materials which exist to be selected.

The best starting point for any critical discussion of *Hard Times* is provided by the editors of the Norton Edition of the novel:

> Many of the most helpful critical discussions of Dickens's other novels have been interpretative, whereas most discussions of *Hard Times* have been primarily evaluative. About none of his novels has there been less agreement. (*Ford and Monod*, 1966, p. 330)

Not to put too fine a point on it, most of these judgements have been harshly antagonistic. George Saintsbury thought it the lowest amongst Dickens's novels; 'good things were buried in a mass of exaggeration and false drawing that one struggles with the book as with a bad dream.' (cited *Churchill*, 1975, p. 95) Stephen Leacock thought it 'half-story, half-sermon, – a large tract of the book is mere trash – the humour is forced ... the pathos verges on the maudlin.' (*Churchill*, p. 95) George Gissing, a keen admirer of Dickens, regarded the novel so lightly, he ignored it. 'Of *Hard Times* I have said nothing; it is practically a forgotten book and little of it demands attention.' (*Ford and Monod*, p. 330)

In this book I have taken up the invitation offered by Ford and Monod and have suspended dealing directly with the question of value. Whereas my survey deals with critics who, inevitably, evaluate the book and why they have evaluated it the way that they do, my appraisal is more concerned with what is in the novel than how good it is. My own view is that the ultimate question of value is not one which literary criticism can satisfactorily conclude because the presuppositions from which criticism argues are themselves open to large, inconclusive dispute, which has little to do with literary matters. Only within a very closely confined, highly specialised, set of criteria can one reach agreements on value, and one suspects the criteria would have to be *so* narrowly defined that what would be left to say would not be worth saying. This is not to say there is no such thing as value, because there is, nor that critical opinions do not have greater or lesser value, because they do, but, rather, to acknowledge that although we use terms of value all the time, only within a very closed field are such terms of value truly meaningful. Literary criticism is not a closed field, but an open landscape.

René Wellek has argued rather adroitly that differences of opinion are not so much due to different responses, but to the selection of different values in the text. (Wellek, p. 51) But this is to push the argument one stage further back to realise that the selection is based upon extra-literary reasons. Contemporary critics who declare themselves feminists or Marxists or deconstructionists hope to more closely define the field, but within each of these broad terms there exists a wide divergence of opinion as to what value is or how it is constituted. Far better to analyse a text for what it is rather than assigning it a place in a hierarchy of authors or texts. What a critic values will inhere in his/her criticism, as much as in any declared intention, and this is why criticism itself needs to be interpreted for its selection of values.

My selection is not quite random. What I have attempted to do with these critical approaches to *Hard Times* is to show how an intermittently continuous development of one major idea has informed the critics. That idea has been projected by the novel itself.

It is a very important idea, but it is also a protean one taking different names. For Dickens himself it was fact and fancy. Some have called it Creativity versus Utilitarianism. It could be called imagination and reason. In its imaged form, it is Coketown and the circus. In character terms it might be Sissy and Bitzer, or Gradgrind and Sleary. One critic has called it 'humanity and system'. My preferred terms are the literary and the sociological imagination. Admittedly, these are rather abstract, but the sheer multiplicity of the polarisations in the novel, as well as the novel's rather abstract quality itself, do justify them, I believe. The novel has always been part of a debate, and what that debate points to is a questioning of the worth of the creative literary imagination, exemplified here by a novel, in a scientific and industrial capitalist society, because this debate is internal to the novel itself. It raises, therefore, important questions for all readers of fiction. Why should we have literary works? Why should we read them? Is the literary imagination relevant in an industrial scientific society? Is not the sociological imagination, my arbitrary term for that which ensures that that society continues to function and materially prosper, really what is important? By exploring the several critical comments in the survey and by my own appraisal I hope to show what sort of answer *Hard Times* might leave us with.

One of the characteristics of *Hard Times* which all commentators have noticed is that:

> any account of Dickens's argument in the novel is bound to come to the conclusion that he attacks an unmanageably large and miscellaneous range of evils (utilitarianism in education and economics, industrial capitalism, abuse of unions, statistics, bad marriage, selfishness, etc.); that he mostly oversimplifies them . . . that he is unclear on what evil causes what other evil. On the other side his proposed palliatives are feeble . . . (*Fowler*, 1983, p. 106)

Because Dickens is so unfocussed (what is *Hard Times* principally about might be a good starting point) critics have often thought it a bad novel. But the argument can be seen in a double context. On the one hand, it is clearly satirical of contemporary society, for which Dickens received considerable criticism. But it is also about a particular way of seeing the world which is in contradistinction to the literary imagination, a way which is exemplified perfectly by Bitzer's rational arguments. In the conflict of the literary and sociological imagination what Dickens is showing is how a particular vision of life is becoming increasingly subject to abstract formalisation, into the narrow and the rigid. Like any writer he is concerned that his way of seeing will be granted tolerance and will endure, but he wrote knowing all too well that the sort of thinking that his novel opposes, Blue Books and 'ologies', was exercising a profound effect.

Hard Times can be seen as the defence of the novel, of literature as a valuable necessity and a valuable professional activity, and is consequently to be judged as such at the very time when a scientific and industrial society made any blithe confidence in such an undertaking impossible. What actually happens in the novel (as opposed to what one might like to think happens in it) is that the text reveals ironies and its indirections so that it becomes not a confident attack on the evils of systematisation, but exhibits instead a crisis in confidence. That doubt is dramatised in the language of the fiction at many points. Even the terms Fact and Fiction are themselves not at all clear.

I believe, therefore, that this novel still has a prescient relevance for us because the larger questions, or the more abstract ones it addresses, are still with us. But I also recognise that *Hard Times* will still not please many. This is a pity because apart from the pleasures which it undoubtedly contains, the reminder of what school can *feel* like, its delicate but penetrating exploration of the callousness of selfishness, the access to Victorian history, and its debates and ideas which it affords in a short and condensed way, it is also, as my epilogue will suggest, a novel which offers a comment on the decade of the 1980s. Some readers do, it is true, find it excessively gloomy. Some no longer wish to read of the heyday of British industrialism. Some find it unfunny (which it certainly isn't). Some, despite its deft economy, find it too long; for those whose only narratorial satisfactions come in the 1 hour 30 minutes of film or the 50 minute television play one can, alas, do nothing. However, one should not read Dickens with cloth ears. He can be, and he is particularly so in this novel, amazingly ironic. He was unafraid to be scornfully bitter about his opponents, usually systems or ideas rather than individual people, despite his reputed generous good nature. Orwell, one of his most sympathetic readers, said that, 'Dickens attacked English

institutions with a ferocity that has never since been approached.'
(*Orwell*, 1970, p. 455) This is marvellously true. Students are often
reluctant to recognise openly what they may feel intuitively, that
novelists and poets can be savagely and violently angry, and yet
wholly serious, beneath their humour.

Part One: Survey

The textual approach

Textual critics concern themselves with the transmission of the physical text from manuscript and notes to the printed versions of the text – usually a book – in which the author's work becomes known to us. The word textual here has a specific meaning; it is not used metaphorically as in theoretical criticism – 'the intertextual' – and it works very much on the basis of an author's declared intentions as these can be gathered from several sources (letters, memoranda, notebooks, etc.). Modern criticism often feels nervous about admitting such evidence as having an authority in the work's interpretation, and whilst not ignoring it completely, may tend to discount it. The method derives from Shakespearian textual bibliography and it deals with the general questions surrounding the condition and production of printed texts as these can be factually verifiable. It works from documentable evidence in other words.

The most famous example of the method applied to nineteenth-century literature is John Butt and Kathleen Tillotson's *Dickens at Work* (1957, 1968), a highly illuminating and fascinatingly detailed study which was designed to serve as a sort of model for editing a nineteenth-century novel. Their chapter on *Hard Times* does not set out to challenge established views of Dickens's worth, or indeed to upset interpretative applecarts. Both authors shared 'a conviction of Dickens's greatness as a creative artist'. (*Butt and Tillotson*, p. 7) What, rather, they were concerned to show was how he responded to the pressures of writing for serial publication. They are concerned not so much with the finished result but with the process of the text at various points as Dickens completes his novels in periodical form before they are issued in volume format. They provide a primary sort of evidence upon which interpretations may be rightly established. If we can learn how Dickens manœuvres his way around the

restrictions placed upon him by meeting deadlines, writing to pre-
cise length, ensuring that certain sections ended with the requisite
climax to keep the readers in suspense, we shall learn something
about how the novels are structured; and indeed we do.

Two things we learn right away are explanations as to why this
novel is shorter than his others, and why it is written in a very
economical sort of manner. (If anyone thinks Dickens after *Bleak
House* (1852–3) had given up on the long novel, *Little Dorrit* (1855–7)
and *Our Mutual Friend* (1864–5) were still to come.) We learn that
Dickens, one of the co-proprietors of the weekly journal *Household
Words*, believed that a story by him 'would make some unheard of
effect', which it certainly did, the circulation of the periodical first
doubling, then quadrupling as the serialisation continued. But the
price which was paid for this was a serious interference with
Dickens's normal writing habits. Throughout, he complained that
the 'sense of restriction never left him'. What he was used to was
writing for monthly periodical publication. The habit was so
ingrained, that we find him making calculations as to how he can
translate his story into 'the old Monthly Nos'. Butt and Tillotson
show us the mechanics of the process.

> One sheet (16 pages of *Bleak House*) will make 10 pages and a
> quarter of Household Words. Fifteen pages of my writing make a
> sheet of *Bleak House*.
> A page and a half of my writing, will make a page of Household
> Words.
> The quantity of the story to be published weekly, being about
> five pages of Household Words, will require about *seven pages and
> a half of my writing*. (*Butt and Tillotson*, p. 202)

But this is more than an insight into the sheer exigencies of being
a professional writer. Working to a weekly rather than a monthly
unit meant that all the genial expansiveness of the large novel had to
be abandoned. Whereas a monthly unit would have consisted of
thirty-two pages, and Dickens would have hoped to include within
that two or three different episodes, he now had to include the same
variety, but with only a quarter of the space. Butt and Tillotson
argue, for instance, that it is 'difficult to believe that in any monthly
novel Dickens would have been content with those mere eight but
sufficient words which set the scene, "a plain, bare, monotonous
vault of a schoolroom".' (*Butt and Tillotson*, p. 203)

Nevertheless, he did not abandon his sense of a monthly unit. It is interesting to learn that in the original manuscript the novel is actually divided into five monthly parts (it ran from 1 April to 12 August 1854), and that these provided him with a sort of skeleton of the novel's progress. In fact, the ending of each monthly section is a significant factor in the novel's design, though both modern readers who read the book in one volume, and the original serial readers, would not have been especially aware of the monthly pattern.

The major division of the novel into 'books', 'Sowing', 'Reaping', 'Garnering', introduces yet another form of cycle, though these sub-headings were not in the original weekly publication. By the time Dickens had thought about them, quite early on as it happened, the serial was under way, and though they coincide with the endings of the second and the fourth monthly parts, they were not really part of the way the original readership would have responded to the novel.

We learn too that a writer's first thoughts may or may not be his last. On the matter of names of characters, always important in Dickens for their onomatopoeic effect, Bounderby was originally 'Bounder', Stephen Blackpool was variously 'John Prodge', then 'Stephen', 'George', 'Old Stephen'. On the other hand, he seems to have hit upon Gradgrind first time, as indeed he did for the names of the Gradgrind children, noting from the start of 'Adam Smith, Malthus, and Jane', that they would have 'no parts to play'. In fact, as we know, Jane is later to play a small part in the reconciliation of Sissy and Louisa. But it is interesting that we are told nothing about the other Gradgrind children in the novel. The most interesting of all the questions of names is what the novel was to be called. Dickens provided Forster with a long list, and then added more in his manuscript.

According to Cocker, Prove It, Stubborn Things, Mr Gradgrind's Facts, The Grindstone, Hard Times, Two and Two are Four, Something Tangible, Our Hardheaded Friend, Rust and Dust, Simple Arithmetic, A Matter of Calculation, A Mere Question of Figures, The Gradgrind Philosophy Fact, Hard-headed Gradgrind, Hard Heads and Soft Hearts, Heads and Tales, Black and White. Butt and Tillotson see the various titles as indicating 'the limits within which the book would move.' (p. 202) But we might also judge that Dickens was unsure even to the point of titles as to what exactly was to be the subject of his novel. Moreover, he did not generally favour long titles, nor did he favour abstract ones. Only *Great Expectations* (1860–1) matches *Hard Times* in abstraction as a title. (Both, incidentally, were unillustrated.)

Dickens seemed to have preferred either people's names, or a specific place or thing. But textual criticism is not merely the recording of fact and documentation, though one needs to read the whole of Butt and Tillotson to appreciate the density and intricacy of their argument. It is also supposition and speculation, as well as critical judgement. Pointing out how Dickens structures the narrative so that the reader is prepared for Bounderby's exposure, by emphasising his mock humility in endless counterpoint with Mrs Sparsit's mock gentility, they comment: 'Here at the very centre of the domination of Fact are people indulging in Fancy, a peculiarly repulsive Fancy maybe, but Fancy still.' (*Butt and Tillotson*, p. 208) This is a crucial aspect of the novel and goes to the very heart of the book's ironies, those supposedly committed to fact are wildly fanciful. My appraisal will try to make sense of this paradox which is central to the book's meaning. Similarly, another judgement which Butt and Tillotson make needs to be considered later in an interpretative context, and that is the use of Sissy to dispose of James Harthouse.

'Sissy, like Jack the Giant-killer, goes resolutely forth . . . and succeeds in touching "him in the cavity where his heart should have been." Both Harthouse and the reader agree that it is "very ridiculous" that a stroller's child should succeed in evicting a parliamentary candidate from his prospective constituency; but that is how things happen in fairy tales, and Dickens could never entirely resist the satisfaction of giving the victory over the forces of evil to the children of light.' (*Butt and Tillotson*, pp. 217–18) They offer a less fanciful explanation by pointing out that Gradgrind and Harthouse are very similar, and since Sissy has punctured Gradgrind's complacency she could do the same for Harthouse.

The question which the 'genetic approach' (another term for textual criticism, though genetic study involves the manuscript as it moves through successive layers of completion) essentially raises is the one of an author's intention. Textual criticism gives priority and authority to what the author says about his own work and what he hopes to do within it. It therefore usually provides a sort of bedrock upon which biographical study often rests, since it too tends to use letters and documents, though a biographer's reading of a text is usually more speculative than a textual critic's. Every biography is of its own time, both in the sense of the known material upon which it can draw, and the critical fashions and ideas which are in place when it is written. It also provides material for a type of historical approach to works in the past which set out to relate them to their own time. Finally, it should be repeated that the exercise of Butt and Tillotson was a prelude to the proper editing of Dickens's works (still in progress), and that they were trying to establish the ground rules for such editions. Theirs represents an approach which is more for the editor than the critic of a text, but good criticism is usually founded on sound knowledge.

The nineteenth century: a social approach

In this section I shall be concerned with those critics of the nineteenth century who do not fit the academic categories that are now common in the institutional discussion of literature. I have called them social critics because not only were they unspecialised in their responses to literature, as indeed to much else, but because their largeness of interest took in society as a whole as well as literature. They could as happily discuss in the same essay important social and economic questions as well as what we would now think of as purely literary ones, such as genre and characters, or whether the latter were realistic or not, and they could do so without feeling any embarrassment that they might be trespassing on areas of expertise outside their own knowledge. Although they often come to different conclusions about the quality of *Hard Times*, for nearly all their criticism is motivated first and foremost by the need to come to a value judgement, they were all middle-class writers of various sorts, and they shared the same anterior beliefs of what literature was and what sort of place it occupied in society. Hence, if a writer wrote badly this was a social error, not merely a literary one. When it came to literature, as with nearly everything else, the Victorian social critic was well fortified by a heavy dose of moral seriousness.

Ruskin

Fortified more than most was John Ruskin, yet his judgement on *Hard Times*, which, in part, is a judgement on Dickens in general, is a wholly sympathetic one. It is worth citing in full because it encapsulates in brief what the critics then, and subsequently, have tended mostly to disagree about:

The essential value and truth of Dickens's writings have been unwisely lost sight of by many thoughtful persons, merely because he presents his truth with some colour of caricature. Unwisely, because Dickens's caricature, though often gross, is never mistaken. Allowing for his manner of telling them, the things he tells us are always true. I wish that he could think it right to limit his brilliant exaggeration to works written only for public amusement; and when he takes up a subject of high national importance, such as that which he handled in *Hard Times*, that he would use severer and more accurate analysis.

The usefulness of that work (to my mind, in several respects the greatest he has written) is with many persons seriously diminished because Mr. Bounderby is a dramatic monster, instead of a characteristic example of a worldly master; and Stephen Blackpool, a dramatic perfection, instead of an honest workman. But let us not lose the use of Dickens's wit and insight because he chooses to speak in a circle of stage fire. He is entirely right in his main drift and purpose in every book he has written; and all of them, but especially *Hard Times* should be studied with close and earnest care by persons interested in social questions. They will find much that is partial, and, because partial, apparently unjust; but if they examine all the evidence on the other side, which Dickens seems to overlook, it will appear, after all their trouble, that his view was finally the right one, grossly and sharply told. (*Ruskin*, 1862, cited *Ford and Monod*, pp. 331–2)

Without offering anything in the way of analyses, and with only the briefest of references to Bounderby and Blackpool, Ruskin's comment nevertheless goes right to the centre of what has been the critical debate over this novel. Contained within the judgement are the two questions, later fragmented into many others, which every critic has in some way had to deal with. The first, which Ruskin expresses in terms of exaggeration or caricature is really a question of the nature of realism. How realist is Dickens? Does he create convincing life-like characters or are they mere caricatures, overly symbolic, with the bad ones stage villains, and the good ones idealised out of all human existence? Can we believe in them? And, if the answer to that fundamental question is in the negative, then how can we think of Dickens as a realistic writer, and, if he is not realistic, then how can he tell the truth? To his contemporary readers, accustomed to the novel as in essence a representational art, realism and truth are intimately bound up with one another.

The second question also turns on the question of truth. Does Dickens know what he is talking about when he criticises society's institutions? Does the powerful expressionist style mask what is at bottom a shallow ignorance of how society works? And, though we may all enjoy the satire, is there not something, ultimately, to use Raymond Williams's term, 'adolescent' about his indignant onslaught on society? Is it actually that he does not understand the complexity of what he is criticising, but nevertheless feels compelled to attack, and because he does not understand, his social critique is in the end vitiated as a serious one?

Needless to say, the jury seems destined to remain out on these questions. Where the critical interest lies is in the ways in which the several critics have approached them. Ruskin's response is what one might call the tolerant allowance. Sympathetic, but by no means uncritical readers of Dickens, tend, as does Ruskin, to allow for the exaggerated effects. They cannot altogether disregard them, but, they make the claim, not unreasonably, that this, in essence, is what Dickens is, and thus one has to accept this sort of art. It is, in other words, a misplaced sort of realism that is being demanded of Dickens. Ruskin cannot quite make up his mind. What he seems to be saying is that the exaggeration and caricature do matter, and that they do not matter. How he resolves this problem is to use the argument of the greater subsuming the lesser, *in the end*. Thus, Dickens's 'view' is finally 'the right one, grossly and sharply told'. But, the non-sympathetic critic who does not grant Dickens a tolerant allowance, would reply that if grossly and sharply told, it cannot be right!

Philip Collins uses exactly the same sort of the greater subsuming the lesser argument as a means of granting the tolerant allowance when he discusses the incident of the flowers on the wall and the lesson in taste in Chapter 2:

> For though Gradgrind's preoccupation with Hard Facts should not be equated with the Utilitarianism of John Stuart Mill, or his father, Gradgrind and his coadjutors *do represent, in a form simplified and heightened after the Dickensian fashion, important impulses in the life and in the schooling of the period*, which masqueraded as 'utilitarian' and which were indeed derived from a crude half-knowledge of Benthamite ideas. (*Collins*, 1963, my italics)

Amongst those nineteenth-century social critics there were several who were not prepared to grant the tolerant allowance of 'a form simplified and heightened after the Dickensian fashion.' Amongst the least tolerant was Harriet Martineau, herself a writer, essayist and social reformer. She may have had personal reasons for disliking the book over and above the inadequacy, as she saw it, of Dickens's meddling where he had no real knowledge. The Norton editors suggest that the satirical reference in Chapter 8 of *Hard Times* to 'leaden little books ... showing how the good grown-up baby invariably got to the Savings-bank, and the bad grown-up baby invariably got transported' is directed at her moral fables extolling the values and virtues of *laissez-faire* economics of which she was such a 'passionate adherent'. Personal rivalry apart, and despite being herself a creator of fictions, she had no time for Ruskin's equivocation. Dickens had set up *Household Words* for popular instruction which involved political philosophy and morality. He is thus accountable for his opinions.

When Dickens was criticised, argues Martineau, his defenders, she notes, always make use of the justification, that 'he was a novelist; and no one was eager to call to account on any matter of doctrine, a very imaginative writer of fiction.' (*Ford and Monod*, 1966, p. 302) He escaped censure with *Bleak House*, but when it comes to *Hard Times* she is not going to accept such a justification. 'On this occasion, again, the plea of those who would plead for Charles Dickens to the last possible moment is that *Hard Times* is fiction.' Having no truck with the Dickens sympathisers, she grants that it is a poor fiction 'in its characters, conversations, and incidents, is so unlike life, – so unlike Lancashire or English life – that it is deprived of its influence.' (p. 302) Pointing out that he gets his facts distorted in his journalism, she advises Dickens that if he is to put himself forward as a social reformer, 'let him do the only honest thing and study both sides of the question he takes up.' In other words if we are to have novels of industrial life, let them be realistic and based upon proper factual bases, and using proper argument. The trouble is, she implies, Dickens is probably not up to it.

If Mr Dickens really believes in such a state of things as he describes, he should not meddle with affairs in which rationality of judgement is required: and if he can be satisfied to represent the great class of manufacturers – unsurpassed for intelligence, public spirit and beneficence – as the monsters he describes, without seeking knowledge of their actual state of mind and course of life, we do not see how he can complain of being himself classed with the pseudo-philanthropists he delights to ridicule. (*Ford and Monod*, p. 304)

Martineau is not against fiction which deals with the industrial life or the people who are involved with it: but what she is so bitterly opposed to are those fictions like *Hard Times* which are distortive of that life.

Is Martineau's judgement a literary one or is it a political one? The social approach would make no distinction. A badly conceived novel, badly conceived because of its perceptions of utilitarian economics, is a badly written book. Assuming the writer sees as he writes and writes as he sees, then, says Martineau, he should leave well alone until he discovers a better way of seeing.

If Harriet Martineau offered a defence against the ravaging of Dickens's satire against the economists and utilitarians of industrial society, James Fitzjames Stephen felt it equally necessary to defend those in public life, the Parliament of which Mr Gradgrind is a member, who also conducted the nation's business on broadly Benthamite lines. Although not yet a judge when he wrote this review, this uncle of Virginia Woolf, and pillar of the Victorian establishment, seems to direct his criticism down from the great height of the Bench. Filled with sarcasm and dripping in authority (it deserves to be read in full), Dickens is judged and sentenced. But there are some useful contributions in this review to the realism, non-realism argument.

Stephen's view represents so much of what is part of that Victorian high seriousness which we associate with figures such as Arnold, though the latter's irony and wit is here replaced by an irritated anger. According to his brother, Stephen believed that a novel should be a serious attempt by a grave observer to draw a faithful portrait of the actual facts of life. A novelist, therefore, who uses the imaginary facts like Sterne and Dickens, as mere pegs on which to hang specimens of his own sensibility and facetiousness, becomes disgusting. His attitude to realism is therefore that it should be conveyed in a language shorn of the very sort of rhetorical excess for which Dickens was famous; inevitably, exaggerated effects would draw his fire. But there was a further reason for his animosity towards the novelist, and that is because Dickens is attacking the institutions and structures of society which Stephen not only cherished, but was so keen a participant in maintaining.

Like Martineau, he finds Dickens ignorant of that which he criticises, but unlike her, he is not prepared to let the argument go at the point of saying Dickens is 'only a novelist'. He takes the novel form, no matter that he sees it in narrowly conceived terms of realism, as a serious matter, and he takes a novelist who has a large readership, and therefore the capacity to influence many, as in very serious error when that writer satirises what he holds most dear. He accuses Dickens of 'moral delinquency' for his untruthfulness. But he goes much further than this when he more or less accuses him of hypocrisy. He complains that whenever Dickens is accused of exaggeration, of being untruthful, the retort is always that 'I am in sport', it is just playfulness. To use the terms of *Hard Times*, 'people must be amused'.

Dickens is the great entertainer. But Stephen will not allow Dickens this form of evasion from his moral responsibilities. One important reason why he will not allow him to evade what Stephen conceives as these responsibilities is that Dickens is an author with mass reader appeal. He is, therefore, 'appealing not to men of sense and cultivation, but to the vast majority of mankind [who] think little and cultivate themselves still less.' To such readers Dickens's satire can only be politically pernicious. With such power and influence must go moral responsibility. 'Who is this man who is so much wiser than the rest of the world that he can pour contempt on all institutions of this country?' (*Collins*, p. 348), thunders Stephen, pointing out that Dickens has never taken part in public administration, and his criticism is therefore no more significant than that of a 'gadfly'. Stephen concedes Dickens's kindheartedness, and his great literary gifts, though all in ways which suggest a badly perverted sense of realism, an 'active fancy, great powers of language, much perception of what is grotesque and melodramatic turn of mind.' (*Collins*, p. 348)

But Dickens's error is all the greater for having these gifts and not using them properly. Stephen's irascibility finally ends in a searingly patriarchal denunciation of Dickens's manliness. The men (they *were* all men) who run the country's administration are not as they are depicted in Dickens's satire of Parliament and the Law (they are not as Dickens would have them in *Hard Times*, serving out the 'little mouldy rations of political economy' or more interested in the cow and the widow's cap than the five killed and the thirty-two injured in a railway accident), but are 'patient, quiet, moderate and tolerant of difference of opinion.' And Dickens, as one who opposes such men, is one of these with a 'feminine, noisy, irritable mind which is always clamouring and shrieking for protection and guidance.' (*Collins*, p. 349) Dickens emerges as a nagging virago to the male principle of authority! He is only capable of 'effeminate understandings'. This is more of an attack on Dickens than specifically on *Hard Times*, and Stephen's threatened patriarchal feelings are not what we might normally think of as nineteenth-century literary criticism. And, like most literary criticism, it tells us as much, if not more, about the critic than the work. But it clearly exposes the raw nerves of those who felt themselves attacked in *Hard Times*.

Stephen really sums up a view which is as patronising as it was common. Authors do harm if they do not tell the truth because the gullible, the uneducated and the innocent will mistake what they say for truth. And the truth, for this sort of sociological mind, can only be expressed in a realistic mode. Whereas Ruskin would probably adhere to the view that it is necessary to tell little lies to arrive at a larger truth, one of the paradoxes of Dickens's sort of art, Stephen would denounce all lies as leading to morally reprehensible thought, and eventually, evil behaviour.

Socio-political approaches: twentieth century

The way in which critics conduct their arguments with an author is usually by opposing the view of a contemporary. Ruskin's seminal comment was as much a response to Stephen as Stephen's was a response to Forster, whose reviews in the *Examiner* acted as a semi-official mouthpiece for the author. By the time we come to George Bernard Shaw, these debates were, as they are for us, firmly historical. The time span between Shaw's Introduction to *Hard Times* and the decade in which the novel appeared was that between our own day and the decade before the Second World War. Nevertheless, Shaw chose as his starting point, not a contemporary Edwardian opinion of Dickens, but Ruskin's. Did Ruskin really have a justification for making *Hard Times* Dickens's best novel prior to 1862? Substituting favourite for best, Shaw thought this opinion not merely a caprice, but had a rational explanation.

Shaw's view is that *Hard Times* was so beloved by Ruskin because it represents one of those works of the nineteenth century which exemplify what amounts to a 'conversion'; revealed during that conversion was 'social sin'. Ruskin saw what Shaw thought Dickens portrayed best in this novel, which was that 'Civilisation itself was a disease, and it was not our disorder that was so horrible, but our order.' *Hard Times* is the decisive break with the cheery, jolly, 'occasionally indignant', but mostly light-hearted Dickens; now he is the author of 'oppressors and victims, oppressing and suffering . . . driven by a huge machinery which ground the people it should nourish and ennoble.' *Hard Times* belongs with Karl Marx, Carlyle, Morris, Carpenter. In this historical placing, Dickens becomes a sort of proto-socialist. Shaw lifts Dickens out of a literary context, and slots him in alongside the great social thinkers and radicals of the nineteenth century. It was a clever, historicising act. In a way, an inspired one, for *Hard Times* in this new perspective became one of the exemplary novels of a whole tradition of left-wing thought. Once Shaw effects this sideways move, he sets out to demonstrate how keenly Dickens diagnoses the disease of civilisation.

'Only a surface failure'

Replying to Ruskin's apparently odd sympathy to this novel, George Bernard Shaw thought that *Hard Times* 'was written to make you feel uncomfortable, and it will make you uncomfortable . . . though it will interest you more, and certainly leave a deeper scar on you than any of its two forerunners.' This discomfort he located in the novel's creation of characters, Gradgrind or Bounderby, whom it was impossible to enjoy in the way we enjoy Pecksniff or Micawber, or the Artful Dodger because they, as Shaw sees them as, are fictional characters who cannot impinge on our lives in the way these figures can, and do.

> England is not full of Micawbers and Swivellers. They are not our fathers and schoolmasters, our employers, our tyrants. We do not read novels to escape from them and forget them: quite the contrary. But England is full of Bounderbys and Podsnaps and Gradgrinds; and we are all up to a quite appalling extent in their power. We either hate and fear them or else we are them, and we resent being held up to odium by a novelist. (*Ford and Monod*, p. 335)

In other words, this Dickens, who has eschewed his humour, has become a sort of sombre realist or satirist who has hit the right note.

Shaw is here arguing for a view of character which emphasises the bleak reality of these characters as against the humorous fictionality almost of earlier ones. This might seem a strange, even a non-sustainable distinction. After all, these are all fictional characters; but the identification of characters with readers by Shaw (who was neither a businessman nor a schoolmaster) proposes that we recognise all too easily the sort of people that this capitalist civilisation has produced, and indeed, holds up as admirable models for behaviour.

Dickens's satire is acutely penetrating because of its realism and the ease with which we can recognise these types, and the values which they endorse and maintain, simplified though they may be. How realistic a novel *Hard Times* is is one of those infinitely elastic questions: realism is never easily defined. But as a satire it relies on the projection of ideas through the actions and thoughts of characters who are plausible and recognisable; they seem part of our experience. Satire, after all, if it is not to descend into whimsey or diverge into fantasy, depends on having some firm, perhaps even grim foothold in reality. It demands that we can apprehend what is being satirised. Whatever the degree of vitriolic tone, satire assumes a knowledge on our part of what the characters in the novel would *seem* to act like: they appear as probable from the perspective which the novelist's viewpoint allows us to have. Satire may be thought of as reductive, but since it usually has some moral idea informing it, it necessarily wishes to reduce the sense of its opposition so that its case can be all the more convincing.

Shaw also drew attention to the problem of realism in the nature of the language. He considers Louisa and Sissy as the two wholly serious characters throughout; both are wholly free of the caricatural. For him, Louisa is a figure of poetic tragedy speaking a language of solemn poetry. Sissy's language, on the other hand, he finds more problematic. If it is unreal it is because Dickens has 'allowed himself to be carried away by the scene into a ridiculous substitution of his own most literary and least colloquial style for any language that could conceivably be credited to Sissy.' (*Ford and Monod*, p. 337)

'Mr Harthouse . . . the only reparation that remains with you, is . . . I am quite sure that you can mitigate in no other way . . .' [p. 255] Shaw comments on this whole scene 'Very Ridiculous' that 'this is the language of a Lord Chief Justice, not of the dunce of an elementary school in the Potteries.' However, he is unbothered by such unrealism, for he continues, 'But this is only a surface failure,

just as the extravagances of Mrs. Sparsit are only surface extravagances.' (*Ford and Monod*, p. 337)

One could add, of course, it is not only Sissy's language which is
remarkable (though the fact she was a dunce at arithmetic is no
reason to believe that she could not have learned, after her years in
Gradgrind's school, to speak in a middle-class educated way), but
her whole psychology.

'Surface extravagance' takes us right back to Ruskin's defence of
caricature. This is merely a 'surface failure'. In other words, we can
accept the convention of Sissy speaking in this way (though we
remain unconvinced when Dickens tries his hand at a working
man's diction with Stephen), because it is merely a convention, just
as we can accept Bounderby's or Gradgrind's or Sparsit's wilder
flights of linguistic fancy, though Dickens can overdo it. Shaw goes
part of the way when he says Dickens's business in life has become
too serious for troubling over the small change of verisimilitude, and
denying himself and his readers, the indulgence of his honour in
inessentials. But who is to decide what or what is not an inessential?
Shaw has his mind very firmly made up when it comes to Dickens's
depiction of Slackbridge. Hence Dickens, with his introduction of a
chairman for the meeting and one who is wholly ineffectual in
controlling it, reveals nothing more than middle-class ignorance and
fantasy, as does Slackbridge himself.

Finally, what makes Dickens a convert, but not a true believer, is
the confrontation of Bounderby and Stephen where Stephen's 'a' a
muddle', is pounced upon by the Bully of Humility:

> 'Of course,' said Mr Bounderby. 'Now perhaps you'll let the
> gentleman know, how you would set this muddle (as you're so
> fond of calling it) to rights.'
>
> 'I donno, sir. I canna be expecten to't. 'Tis not me as should be
> looken to for that, sir. 'Tis them as is put ower me, and ower aw
> the rest of us. What do they tak upon themseln, sir, if not to do't?'
> [p. 181]

This, contends Shaw, is Dickens's failure. Here he turns his back on
the working classes, and turns his back on Democracy (Shaw's
capital). Nowhere does Dickens appeal to the working classes to take
their fate into their own hands and try 'the democratic plan'.
Indeed, again and again it is to the ruling classes that Dickens
makes his appeal.

This specialist reading of *Hard Times* is that Dickens has his heart in the right place, but at the final moment, he is no different from the Tory idealisms of Carlyle and Ruskin whose faith is also in the aristocracy remaining the masters of the people.

Shifting the argument

It is customary in the history of Dickens criticism to place alongside one another, Edmund Wilson's *The Two Scrooges* (1939) and George Orwell's *Charles Dickens* (1940). Both were written at a time when Dickens was neither fashionable, nor respectable, in the academic world. Both were attempts to rehabilitate Dickens as a great artist and social critic. As Wilson so nicely put it:

> Dickens had no university education, and the literary men from Oxford and Cambridge, who have lately been sifting fastidiously so much of the English heritage, have rather snubbingly let him alone. The Bloomsbury that talked about Dostoevsky ignored Dostoevsky's master, Dickens. (*Wilson*, 1961, p. 1)

Even the main facts of Dickens's life, for so long concealed, and upon which Wilson was to base so much of his critical approach, had only been released by 'doddering Dickens fanciers' (*Wilson*, p. 2). To combat this snobbish rejection of a powerful writer, and to release Dickens from a status of a well-loved, but generally ignored national institution, Wilson produced a masterly study of Dickens using a method of psycho-biographical criticism which related the life and the work in a new way. Much of this feelingly written account has little direct relevance to *Hard Times* because for Wilson the dominating image, and indeed, experience of Dickens's life, was the prison; and whereas *Hard Times* does have its stultifying and suffocating confinement of a small number of characters in a small concentrated location, Wilson was concerned with fictional prisons, not metaphorical ones.

There is no need to push the analogy of, say, Mr Gradgrind's model school, or Stephen's factory, as a metaphor for confinement, because there are sufficient prisons elsewhere in Dickens which make the case more clearly. Wilson's thesis is larger than merely pointing to the prison image, though; it is really a way of bringing back to criticism's sifted fastidiousness important biographical material interpreted in a large way and intellectually secure. It generated a considerable amount of criticism, much of it American, and its insights are still being followed up.

How important is biography? Some critical approaches, especially those fashionable at the time of Wilson's essay, positively eschewed it. Biography was illegitimate evidence for what a text meant; in some critics' approaches to texts it was dismissed as 'gossip'. New Criticism (see next section) has been extraordinarily severe on admission of its evidence to the interpretation of meanings, though Historical Criticism has always used it. Deconstructive criticism is varied enough to include those who are willing to entertain its information, and those who still follow a strict New Critical line. Like so much criticism it very much depends in whose hands it is being used. In Wilson's it amplifies meaning and aids interpretation because it not only accounts for why Dickens chooses the subjects he does, but why he writes about them in certain ways. It is not merely a matter of content, but actual imaginative perception.

Hard Times, for instance, would provide a good example of how the personal obsession is broadened out to become a matter of social and political importance if we take the social 'issue' of divorce. Stephen cannot obtain one and neither can Louisa, both victims of the breakdown of marriage in a society in which divorce is prohibitively expensive at a cost of £1,000. Now although Dickens did not separate officially from his wife until 1858, it is clear that his marriage had broken down much earlier than this. A psycho-biographical approach might ask if the two breakdowns of marriage, and the characterisation of the dotty, weak-minded and wholly in-effectual Mrs Gradgrind, the epitome of insipid self-effacement and the victim of both Gradgrind's and Bounderby's bullying, are not to be related to the psycho-drama Dickens himself was undergoing at the time. It is not a direct one-to-one relationship that this sort of critical approach is interested in, i.e. Mrs Dickens *is* Mrs Gradgrind, but the ramifications of that equivalence, such that Dickens would appear in the Gradgrind role, and thus the novel is as much about his terrible guilt as about a weak-willed wife bullied by her genius husband.

Wilson's essay, though itself remarkably free of jargon, neverthe-less opened up Dickens criticism (to minds less subtle than his) to the worst excesses of psycho-analytic study. Much the greater part of this was American, an inevitable difference given that psycho-analysis occupies a different place in the national culture to that which it occupies in Britain.

A political note: George Orwell

Like Wilson, Orwell was prepared to make a case for Dickens when it was singularly unfashionable to do so amongst the intelligentsia. Both writers, incidentally, had more than their fair share of that curious, if nevertheless healthy, sceptical hostility which afflicts the anti-intellectual intellectual. But whereas Wilson argues for the seriousness of Dickens, making him out to be a sort of honorary master of European melancholia, Orwell stresses his great gifts as a popular, and an *English* popular, writer. Orwell wanted to inject his own brand of political literary criticism into a re-assessment, thereby rescuing the novelist from his appropriation by, on the one hand, G. K. Chesterton, who had written a series of Introductions for the Everyman edition, and on the other, T. A. Jackson, who had claimed him for the Marxist cause. The former, according to Orwell, meant a Dickens 'credited with Chesterton's own individual brand of mediaevalism', which was a more charitable judgement than Wilson's, who also mentioned Jackson, but who characterised Chesterton's criticism as displaying 'that peculiar pseudo-poetic booziness which verbalises with large conceptions and ignores the most obtrusive actualities.' (*Wilson*, p. 2) Orwell set about his rescue by pointing out that Dickens was neither a Christian apologist nor a Marxist ideologue. Neither was he a proletarian writer, another of Chesterton's critical follies. Orwell's essay, rich in its personal enthusiasms, and secure in its confident knowledge of the Dickens *œuvre*, concludes that Dickens is not to be claimed as a socialist writer either. But if he is not a socialist, then what is he and why is it still important to read his novels?

Dickens is irremediably bourgeois, but he is also subversive; he is a radical, even a rebel, the last a point on which Orwell and Wilson concur (Wilson thought Dickens was always haunted by the images of the criminal and the rebel). Where, therefore, does he stand, socially, morally and, most importantly of all, politically? For, despite Dickens's radicalism, and his obvious sympathy for the non-governing classes, a novel such as *Hard Times* is no socialist tract for the times, but is, if anything, *pro*-capitalist because Dickens does not set out to destroy the structure of society, nor the system by which that structure is held in place, but to reform the individuals within it by showing a change of heart through personal discovery.

Orwell offers the usual severe socialist critique at this point: 'a change of heart is in fact *the* alibi of people who do not wish to endanger the status quo.' (*Orwell*, p. 469) This is the crucial distinction between the socialist and the non-socialist writer, and why Dickens cannot be classed as the former, despite Macaulay's refusal to review a novel which was nothing more than 'sullen socialism'. He, too, got it wrong. Orwell is not saying that Dickens is admiring of that which he criticises, for that would be to make him a reactionary humbug, which Orwell feels he certainly is not; but that, despite his seemingly comprehensive critique of society, it is, in reality, only one which hits at the surface of things. Hence, it is not what Bounderby and Gradgrind do that is important, but the social system which is at fault. Gradgrind, after all, is a reformed character at the end, and Bounderby is truly humbled. The system, however, continues, and Dickens can project no way out of that.

Orwell's perspective is, in fact, copybook vulgar Marxism; the socio-economic system is put first, and the individual within it second. Vulgar Marxism, if it is not too much of a parody to describe it as such, always maintains that a bourgeois work of literature does not provide within it a revolutionary alternative to the capitalist society of which it is offering a critique; therefore it fails. On this reckoning, ninety-nine per cent of literature is a failure. Moreover, this ideological purity of view seems to assume that once social classes are abolished people will stop being selfish, nasty, egotistical, greedy, homicidal, because these are the products of a divided capitalist society. Despite the claims of a humanised Marxism, this does seem a very naive view of human psychology and behaviour, which literature itself continually disproves. Orwell himself did not altogether go along with this, but he could use it when it suited him, as here. Disclaiming Dickens as a socialist, Marxist or otherwise, he is more or less repeating what Shaw, who was a much cleaner socialist thinker than Orwell, had said when he shows Dickens's failure with his description of the trades union. Had Dickens shown them in a positive light, as spearheading democratic methods, and had Stephen Blackpool not been a union exile, then a socialist view could have been seen to emerge. But, of course, Dickens dismisses Slackbridge's verbal monomania as much as he condemns Bounderby's hypocrisy.

But Orwell wants to go further than Shaw. His problem is that for him there is a terrible dichotomy between his aesthetic and his political preferences. It is, after all, in this essay that he makes his famous declaration that 'all art is propaganda' but that 'not all propaganda is art.' (p. 492) Orwell actually *likes* Dickens, but he also seems acutely aware that he must not be seen to be indulging in some sort of unsocialist appraisal. His major specific criticism of *Hard Times*, is that when Dickens describes any scene he can only describe the appearance of things, their surface, and not the actual underlying process. He also finds Dickens strangely 'unmechanically minded', but, rather, preoccupied with non-functional description, even though what he is ostensibly describing is machinery and the industrial process. For evidence, he adduces the longest description in the novel, Chapter 5, 'The Key-note':

> It was a town of red brick, or of brick that would have been red if the smoke and ashes had allowed it; but, as matters stood it was a town of unnatural red and black like the painted face of a savage. It was a town of machinery and tall chimneys, out of which interminable serpents of smoke trailed themselves for ever and ever, and never got uncoiled. It had a black canal in it, and a river that ran purple with ill-smelling dye, and vast piles of buildings full of windows where there was a rattling and a trembling all day long, and where the piston of the steam engine worked monotonously up and down, like the head of an elephant in a state of melancholy madness. It contained several large streets all very like one another, and many small streets still more like one another, inhabited by people equally like one another, who all went in and out at the same hours, with the same sound upon the same pavements, to do the same work, and to whom every day was the same as yesterday and tomorrow, and every year the counterpart of the last and the next. [p. 65]

This is not a description as seen from the 'inside', says Orwell, but a description from 'the consumer angle': it is not as an engineer or a cotton broker would see it. Indeed, this evocation of a Lancashire town is nothing more than how a slightly disgusted southern visitor would view the place. Of course, the engineer or cotton broker would miss the impressionist touch of the 'elephant' in a state of 'melancholy madness'.

Orwell's reading of this passage is a curiously selective one. Partly this is because he makes no attempt to relate the passage to the rest of the novel (monotony and mad elephants recur as leitmotif), but, instead, simply uses it as an example of Dickens's descriptive powers as if these were unanchored in any context. One must also remember that Dickens has less than his usual amount of space in which to

work, and that an impressionist sketch is all that is possible. But
more than that, it seems to me that Orwell completely mistakes the
tone of the piece, as well as its purpose. 'Slightly disgusted' is a
fastidiousness that diminishes the passage's effect. 'The painted face
of a savage', the 'serpents of smoke', and the melancholy mad
elephants evoke the notion of a sort of hellish jungle rather than a
city.

Dickens's deep animistic impulses are to populate this mechanical
place with humans who act less than human, because of the
drudgery of their lives, and to make the mechanical, the pistons, the
brick, take on an animal life of their own. This is precisely *not* seeing
the surface of things, but the creation of a heavily interpreted scene
for Dickens's purposes. And it does very much describe a process,
though a psychological if not an industrial one, in which the spirit
and animation of life is transferred, as in some vast draining project,
to what should properly be the unanimated. Though this is not a
description which would satisfy any trades description act of factory
and street scene, it is certainly not a static or passive one; there is an
active process very much going on.

Behind Orwell's critique there seems to lurk the old idea that the
novelist does not know what he is talking about, but has to make do
with a few sketchy remarks that could have applied to any city: they
are not authentically specific to an industrial town. This criticism is
less easily met for whilst this description is part of the imaginative
whole of *Hard Times* where it works its rhetorical effects in conjunction with others, it is clearly not industrial life 'from the inside'. But
for Orwell to note this absence is part of his case against Dickens
that he cannot write inwardly of the urban, industrial proletariat,
demonstrated by the solitary portrait of an industrial worker
throughout Dickens's work, of Stephen Blackpool (Orwell here
reveals the chauvinist view of socialism which is that women who
work, do not count; Rachael is also an industrial worker).

It is not intricate and lengthy description of machines which
would make an industrial novel convincing 'from the inside'. Most
employees in a cotton town would no more have known how a
machine is built or what makes it work scientifically than they would
have known how to proof-read one of Orwell's novels. What an
industrial novel could show was how people's lives are dominated by
and used by machines which are in the ownership of other people:
the consequences of which are alienation and powerlessness. What
Dickens is attempting to show, and what Orwell feels he is not

altogether successful at, is what it 'feels' like to be part of the industrial life. And behind this assessment is the much larger question of the relation of literature to politics, an approach which not only informs nearly everything which Orwell writes, but which has influenced subsequent critics. Williams, Craig and Lerner have all plaintively lamented that *Hard Times*, in Craig's formulation, is a symptom of 'the great industrial novel that never did get written', even if 'Coketown' is 'the classic name for the early industrial city.' (*Craig*, p. 36)

Yet despite this failure of the attempt to create a convincing industrial novel, Orwell still finds in Dickens's favour as a 'revolutionary writer'. What Orwell attempts to do is to broaden out the term 'political' so that even though Dickens is above all 'a moralist', 'it is not at all certain that a merely moral criticism of society may not be just as revolutionary – and revolution, after all, means turning things upside down.' This is a bold move on Orwell's part, given the circumstances and the time in which it was written, but it is an approach which increasingly underpins much of contemporary critical thought. Orwell feels apologetic when he remarks that 'Blake was not a politician, but there is more understanding of the nature of capitalist society in a poem like "I wandered through each chartered street" than in three quarters of Socialist literature.' (*Orwell*, pp. 468–9) In post-structuralist criticism now, such a statement is hardly likely to raise a critical eyebrow. Indeed, to find a critical interpretation which is *not* politically motivated would be the exception; it has almost become a self-evident truth that the word political has been stretched so that it no longer means something prosaic like political parties, but something much wider, more diffuse, often theoretical, such as the power relations which exist in society, and those in the discourses of society. Contemporary criticism is likely to go the other way than Orwell and see *everything* as political, which can sometimes produce a certain loss in sensitivity to language and to its ambiguity.

Often, where the problem lies, and *Hard Times* in its 'failure' as an industrial novel is concerned not with language, is with the subject matter of novels. Modern novels are often novels of interior consciousness, their social remit the strained and attenuated human and psychic relations of a fairly distinct minority in society: the highly literate, over-articulate, specifically non-industrial, Oxbridge-educated middle classes. Their public faces are turned inwards; their authors, critical though they may be of life, simply accept the bourgeois condition as the natural, or the preferred state of things. They are not unfeeling people, nor are they not on the side of justice against injustice, or the powerless against the powerful, but neither are they revolutionary either.

Orwell's view of *Hard Times*, because it is his view of Dickens generally, is that in this novel its author may have simulated revolutionary sentiments, but, in the end, his view is to be identified with that of the 'nineteenth-century liberal.' And yet, of course, *Hard Times* is not like a modern novel. Its scope is large. It deals with political affairs, economic powers, trade unions, Parliament, divorce laws, the railways, industrialism, the education system, and the ideological half-thinking which informs society at the time of its writing, which goes under the name of Benthamite Utilitarianism.

Orwell's approach gets him into some confusions about the nature of how political a novel is because often he is concerned with the content rather than (at least as it emerges in his criticism) with the overall vision. Content analysis, as for instance with his 'there is only one industrial worker in Dickens' is a mode often used in political criticism, but it is about as literary a judgement as remarking that there is only one Danish prince in Shakespeare. This is to seek in literature accurate representation of the numerical distribution as it exists in the society from which that work of literature appears. Fortunately or unfortunately, depending on your point of view, literature does not guarantee to provide this sort of ideal representativeness.

New criticism: the great debate; one Cambridge don

In terms of its evaluation, *Hard Times* is doubly unusual. First, it has a special place in the Dickens canon: short and least loved, it is the runt of a sprawling litter. Second, by an accident of critical circuitry, it occupies a special place in the general twentieth-century history of critical debate of the English novel, and that uniquely, because F. R. Leavis, the single most influential critic of the century's middle years, specifically chose it as a 'serious work of art' (1948), from a novelist he deliberately excluded from the Great Tradition (of English novelists).

On the face of it, this was a judgement as narrow and perverse as it was devastating. Leavis argued that 'the adult mind doesn't as a rule find in Dickens a challenge to an unusual and sustained seriousness', and that whilst he was willing to concede that he was a 'genius' and amongst the permanent classics (two honours that would satisfy most people, one would have thought), the genius is, alas, only that 'of a great entertainer'. (*Leavis*, p. 29) Leavis did not say Dickens was not worth reading – he especially disclaimed that judgement – nor did he fail to acknowledge Dickens's influence on the novel subsequently. What he did say, though, was that *Hard Times* was a masterpiece of a writer who did not belong to the tradition he was attempting to establish on his own criteria of moral seriousness. Years later Leavis collaborated with his wife, Q. D. Leavis on a book on Dickens in which he more or less rejected the parsimony of the earlier overall judgement.

What is the Leavisite approach?

There are two ways of characterising Leavis's approach to literary texts. One is to say that Leavis is a 'New Critic'; he belongs to those who see literature as independent of its sociological anchorage, its historical dimensions, or indeed, the historical conditions under which the critics write; instead, his concern is with the 'words on the page', and that novels and poems are organic wholes or structures, and the highly sensitivised critic is, by practice in practical criticism and experience, able to analyse texts, and come to judgements upon them so as to place them in a hierarchy of which the single most important underlying quality is the moral seriousness of the work under scrutiny. The critic disregards biographical chit-chat, and he shows little concern for historical conditions. Biographical evidence may be interesting, it may even be used now and then, but the work itself is what we judge by. New critics, moreover, make no attempt to place the work as belonging to a specific historical time. They are much more concerned with aesthetic and technical effects of a work: its creation of character, its use (or parody) of a genre, its internal organisation so as to produce artistic unity.

In essence, the New Critic judges a novel or poem as a work of art. The greater the number of 'effects' – these can be anything which the critic chooses – the greater the work. American 'New Criticism' liked at one point to formalise the looseness of the aesthetic values chosen, and championed what became almost the four Gospels of criticism; irony, ambiguity, paradox and tension. A work which did not display these characteristics within its form could not expect to receive an approving value judgement. But, needless to say, what are in fact conditions of language, and ones which are particularly attractive to the modern mind, did mean that certain authors of the past must necessarily be relegated. Eventually, New Criticism moved on; it relaxed its criteria, and authors who had been down-classed, essentially the Romantics, were brought back into the fold. But once a critical method designed to sift and separate could, in versatile hands, be used of every writer of any period, it could no longer serve its original intention, which was to distinguish the good from the better.

Leavis was very much concerned with distinguishing one work from another so as to arrive at a hierarchy of judgement; but there was another side to him, one which specifically chose to reject the systematic formalism (another word for the New Critical approach) of American criticism, and which was part of a much older view of the critic, that of the moral appraiser. In this, he is no different from the sort of nineteenth-century social critics such as Harriet Martineau, or twentieth-century ones such as Bernard Shaw. The problem with the Leavisite approach is that whilst some (though not the majority) of the practical criticism is sometimes interesting and insightful, and whilst the moral statements of a generalised nature are plausible and discussable (whether one agrees with them or not), the relationship between these two aspects in Leavis's criticism is one of disjunction rather than coincidence. The Leavis approach is to work from the general to the supposedly concrete and back again, but because he has neither a well-developed theory in terms of the literature form, nor in a theory of language, what should be evidential material to support the generalisations often appears in large undigested passages, which the critic-reader is meant to see as making the link. Supposedly, a Leavisite approach to literature asks the question of the fellow critic, 'This is so, isn't it?' What it really asks is 'Why is it so? How is it so?'

The Leavisite approach to Hard Times

Leavis's famous essay is called 'An Analytic Note', though it begins not with dispassionate analysis, but with a rhetorical provocation:

Hard Times is not a difficult work; its intention and nature are pretty obvious. If then, it is the masterpiece I take it for, why has it not had general recognition? To judge by the critical record, it has had none at all. If there exists anywhere an appreciation, or even an acclaiming reference, I have missed it. In the books and essays on Dickens, so far as I know them, it is passed over as a very minor thing; too light and insignificant to distract us for more than a sentence or two from the works worth critical attention! (*Leavis*, p. 249)

Leavis is making several claims at once. Firstly, he claims it is a masterpiece, a phrase which is never satisfactorily explained or justified, although the whole essay is really an attempt to justify the use of the word. Secondly, he simultaneously attacks those who have read Dickens and those who have not, the first because they have failed to see the quality of what they read, and the latter because they have blindly overlooked what is so stunningly obvious. Notice the way Leavis shifts from the 'intention and nature' of *Hard Times*, which he says are 'obvious', to the recognition, which should be obvious too. A work may be obvious and have a clear intention, yet its value may be obscure. Leavis elides both sets of values so that any reader who has failed to see the conjunction is a lesser reader.

Then, there is the tone and sentiment of this passage, very typical of the remainder of the essay, as we shall see, but which is worth remarking on. One is never sure whether this rhetoric is simple bluff or nervous arrogance. The 'critical record' is taken as given and known. No acknowledgement of its content or its conflicts is made. So, without knowing what it may contain, Leavis can assure his readers he is hardly to be blamed for not finding an appreciation or even an acclaiming reference anywhere. The implication, which is false, is that Leavis, a mature scholar, has looked but failed to discover any critics in favour of *Hard Times*. He clearly has not looked very hard since Ruskin and Shaw are hardly obscure precursor figures. One is led to believe that Leavis's judgement arrives fully formed, outside of history, outside of any critical tradition, a pure disembodied sensibility responding to the text without any intervening critical history. One other rather small point worth mentioning is the way that Leavis switches from 'I' to 'us', when he is still really talking about 'I'.

Leavisite practical criticism

So much, one would want to conclude, for the rhetoric. But, since the essay is written throughout in this elusive style, one has to make

considerable allowances for what Leavis *is* trying to say. This is
paradoxical since, on more than one occasion, Leavis speaks of the
novel representing the obvious. What, then, does Leavis *do* with the
text of *Hard Times*? He chooses certain scenes or passages to
illustrate what he wants to say, and a good instance is provided by
the interrogation of Sissy in Chapter 2, from the insensitive 'Girl
number twenty' [p. 49] down to 'Thus (and much more) Bitzer'
[p. 50]. Leavis builds up his argument concerning this scene by
pointing out various generalities, such as that Dickens is for once
possessed by 'a comprehensive vision, one in which the inhumanities
of Victorian civilisation are seen as fostered and sanctioned by a
hard philosophy, the aggressive formulation of an inhumane spirit',
that Gradgrind introduces the utilitarian spirit into everything he
does, at home and school, and that Bounderby 'is Victorian rugged
individualism.'

Having offered one or two further ways in which the Victorian
view of Utilitarianism is used, he comments 'all this is obvious
enough'. We are, therefore, now ready to see what is not obvious
enough. We come now to the 'art', 'the full critical vision, the
stamina, flexibility combined with consistency, and the hitherto
unacknowledged credit.' Sissy is then interrogated and Bitzer proves
his superiority, but not at the expense of Dickens's irony. After citing
the passage, Leavis offers no linguistic analysis of it. And what has
happened to all those aesthetic terms of vision, stamina, flexibility
(drawn from the world of athletics – horse-riding perhaps – rather
than art criticism)? They have disappeared, for the paragraph after
the citation begins, 'Lawrence, himself, protesting against harmful
tendencies in education, never made the point more tellingly.' But
why invoke D. H. Lawrence to prove what the passage is meant to
prove? Moreover, despite Lawrence's distinctive contribution to
thinking about the educational system, Dickens wrote more about
education than D. H. Lawrence. Leavis thinks Lawrence is a greater
writer than Dickens, as he is entitled to, but Dickens surpasses
Lawrence for his contribution to education.

How bizarre this judgement is or this method of comparison is,
can be tested by reversing it. Imagine praising Lawrence because in
Lady Chatterley's Lover he approached the problem of a failed,
sexually unfulfilled marriage by invoking the loveless match of
Louisa and Bounderby. Comparisons can cut both ways. One
simply does not need the invocation of D. H. Lawrence to demonstrate anything at all. Nor is this an aberration, for after more or less

ignoring the passage he has used to come to a conclusion (which is no more than that Sissy is a poetic symbol, part of 'the poetically creative operation of Dickens's genius', and not a mere conventional persona) we are back to 'the essentially Laurentian suggestion about the dark-eyed and dark-haired girl' contrasted with Bitzer's colour-less complexion which is a manifestation of 'the thin-blooded, quasi-mechanical product of Gradgrindery'. (*Leavis*, pp. 253–4) Sissy, is then, equated with the 'life that is lived freely and richly from the deep instinctive and emotional springs' (*Leavis*, p. 254), which seems a little pagan-like for little Sissy. Nor can Lawrence be left alone, for two pages or so later, Dickens is to be compared with him, yet again. Leavis is here arguing the value of the circus as against the cold bleakness of Coketown, its degradation of life, not merely because the working conditions are so harsh, but because the overall informing ideas of society make it a terrible place. To prove his point (in itself hardly a complex one), we have the passage from *Lady Chatterley's Lover* of the view from the car as it ploughs its way uphill through Tevershall. After a quotation at length, we are told 'Dickens couldn't have put it in just those terms, but the way in which his vision of the horse riders insists on their gracious vitality implies that reaction.' (*Leavis*, p. 256) So now, having been compared three times to D. H. Lawrence, we are to take it as no accident that the method, if there is a method, is that Dickens's effects, particularly in his creation of life-affirming symbolism, are to be compared with Lawrence's (already proved, somewhere else) and not found want-ing.

But juxtaposing the two passages *proves* nothing: nor does it demonstrate anything, except that Leavis finds the two comments on industrial civilisation (separated by nearly seventy years one has to say) alike. But why they are alike, apart from superficial similarities, and how they are alike, and more importantly, where they differ, is not discussed. Lawrence is simply a bench-mark and Dickens is to be measured against him. All that needs to be said on industrial civilisation has been said by Lawrence (chronological development often goes haywire with New Critics) but Dickens did precede Lawrence in the depiction of city and industry as urbanisa-tion advanced.

But even if allowance is made for the vaguenesses and impreci-sions at the local level of Leavisite discourse, it is still difficult to summarise how the process of criticism works. What, instead, remain are various judgements against which the reader may test his own opinions. When Leavis does mention language, all he can do is fall back on what was one of the nineteenth century's most tired clichés – the comparison with Shakespeare. 'Dickens is a great poet: his endless resource to felicitously varied expression is an extraordinary responsiveness to life.' (*Leavis*, p. 272) Where Dickens is seen to fall down is in his description of trade unionism, and his depiction of Stephen Blackpool, both of which are not good (i.e. accurate) typifications. Nor is his description of Parliament as a dust heap in any way a sign of political understanding. But, says Leavis, faults as these are, they are still adequate for his purpose (the understanding of Victorian civilisation), and the justice and penetration of his criticism are unaffected. Here then, we are back to shades of Ruskin's judgement.

But if Leavis does leave a trail in this attempt to prove Dickens's imaginative genius is here at full stretch, it is that he sees the novel as a 'moral fable', which he glosses as 'in it the intention is peculiarly insistent, that the representative significance of everything in the fable – character, episode and so on – is immediately apparent as we read.' In other words, the characters are symbolic, and what they symbolise, Leavis's essay attempts to amplify. (*Leavis*, p. 250)

But if the representative significance is 'immediately apparent', there is no need to write critical articles about that. Or, going back to the rhetoric at the start, is such intention only immediately apparent to this reader, and not other readers, to whom he will now explain it?

Other terms, such as 'astonishing and irresistible richness of life', or Dickens's characters as 'unquestionably real' (the unquestionably wiping out what all Dickens critics have often found so troublesome), 'vital human impulse' and 'vital human needs', are all part of the Leavisite private diction; they appear as terms of approbation rather than critical concepts.

In summary, the Leavisite view works by forceful rhetoric and vigorous assertions of judgements. That Leavis is so difficult to summarise is because he does not really deal in ideas, or concepts, in his approach, but in a sympathetic championing rhetoric. When one does have specific ideas which can be challenged, they have been. One is Leavis's characterisation of the novel as a moral fable: the second has been the value he gives to the circus in the novel, and this, though often found wrong headed, has been a contribution to extended debate.

Leavis raises the question of whether or not Dickens's treatment of the circus is an example of a symbolism sentimentally false? Were these people really not above a little sharp practice? Is Dickens drunk with a moral enthusiasm? The horse riding presents no such case he concludes. Dickens does not give a misleading representation of human nature. (*Leavis*, p. 257) Sleary, described rather fetchingly by Leavis as 'game-eyed, brandy-soaked, flabby-surfaced' (*Leavis*, p. 258), nevertheless suffices for what is to be the humane, anti-utilitarian positive. This then is the symbolic, representative argument again. Realism does not matter, because the symbolic will do its work.

And, finally, what the Leavis essay argues is that Dickens works very much in what we would now call mixed modes; there is conventional novel narrative, there is dramatic satire, there is humour, there is pathos, there is a mixture of elements. Leavis does not categorise these systematically, but he points to them, and this is a refreshing, liberating view to take of the novel, even though, of course, it could apply just as much to other works of Dickens, which he disregards.

How can one characterise the Leavis approach? One way is to see it as primarily indexical rather than analytical. Leavis points his readers in a certain direction by the use of long quotations which he rarely bothers to linguistically analyse, and a vigorous, assertive championing, in this case of the symbolic typicality of the characters and scenes of the novel, but he never demonstrates any close textual reading as a process which provides evidence. In a way, it is as if there is missing from the argument a middle term between the selection of quotation, and the final judgements. Some might argue that this is a measure of Leavis's tact, allowing the student-critic to insert himself into that missing space, to carry out the work of practical criticism for himself, and then see if his conclusions match Leavis's. Others would argue that it is what is missing that vitiates any claim on Leavis's part to be a sort of systematic-thinking critic; but that he is in effect a deeply impressionistic one, whose real reasons for judgement are not in the analysis he gives us, but lie elsewhere in some private moral perspective, which he never fully or satisfactorily articulates.

Leavis created something of a *cause célèbre* with this re-assessment of *Hard Times*. Critics, who had either a stronger sense of history and of chronology, and those whose ideas of symbolism in literature were more developed, responded strongly.

A rejoinder to Leavis

Still snugly within the formalist fold, David M. Hirsch was not prepared to allow Leavis's cavalier assessment of *Hard Times*'s value to go unchecked. Formalism for him means the judgement of a work of art as a work of art, which was very much the New Critical point of view. Leavis's championing of *Hard Times* is false because Leavis, with his moral preoccupations, permits the 'ethos of industrialism' to outweigh what should be a judgement on aesthetic grounds: and hence *Hard Times* is 'one of Dickens's dullest and least successful books' (*Ford and Monod*, p. 372). Hirsch does not deny the relationship of art to morality, but he does deny that Leavis knows what they are. It is quite simply done. Hirsch takes the passages selected by Leavis and opines how badly written they are. Thus the novel is a bad one and Leavis's judgement is therefore wrong.

Moreover, since the judgement is based upon the dynamic relationship between moral and artistic problems, and these in Leavis's case are hazy, the criticism is deficient. Hence, Leavis's inability to see the complexity and ambiguity (key terms for the New Critic) in the symbolism and the imagery. Hirsch matches Leavis's euphoria of praise with a ringing catalogue of just about every deficiency a novel could possess, and a critic looking for things to denigrate could possibly include: 'bad writing', 'bad taste', 'superficiality', 'superficial rhetoric', writing that is 'embarrassingly obvious', 'excessive', 'trite'. As for the dramatic meeting of Louisa and Sissy, which Leavis makes much of, Hirsch finds no power, no mystery, no engagement, just the 'wallowing in the aqueous effusions of a pair of frustrated females'. (*Ford and Monod*, p. 371) 'What is so appalling about Louisa is her hollowness, her suffering.' The good characters, Sissy and Louisa are indeed, feeble-minded, and Dickens intends them to be so. Commenting on a passage in which Sissy recalls seeing her father angry and beating the dog Merrylegs, Hirsch's criticism soars into an empyrean of abuse:

> The problem here is not only sentimentalism, but bad writing and bad taste. If there is any ingenuity or inventiveness it is in Dickens managing to cram so many clichés into one paragraph: the failing performer (let's have a benefit for Judy Garland), the abused pet, the cruel then repentant master, the kindly long suffering daughter, the invocation to Heaven, the cruel kind master-father grovelling wetly in his own tears, being licked by his bleeding dog. (*Ford and Monod*, p. 372)

This is all good knockabout stuff. His final point, that he is not quarrelling with Dickens's sentimentality or, indeed, with Dickens, but with Leavis's 'unkind' criticism that gives this book so high a place in the Dickens canon, is slightly ingenuous, since it is Dickens's conventions of sentimentality he clearly does *not* like; but that said, this is very much an attack on the *Hard Times* defenders, of whom Leavis is the exemplar.

Hirsch's method, like Leavis's, suffers from exactly the same problem that if you select any passage, you can prove what you like about the passage, but this is no guarantee that it will have this 'effect' when read, or that the passage is typical or representative of the rest of the book. And, in a novel of mixed modes, as *Hard Times* very much is, combining fairy tale, naturalistic prose, stagey theatrical dialogue as well as caricature and satire, it is much easier to choose the passage that meets one's critical needs. One of the problems of the New Critical approach is that it was originally designed to work on short poems in which the work could be there in front of you, like a fourteen-line sonnet. You could, therefore, refer backwards and forwards to the whole and the part. But with a long novel this is clearly impossible, local passages selected for evidence prove very problematic to use in terms of aesthetic argument, as opposed to, say, ideological argument about a text.

A theory of organic unity should, of course, get rid of the problem, since it believes the part is reflected in the whole, and the whole in the part, but this runs up against serious objections in long, rambling nineteenth-century novels which often, though very good, will not fit this formalist aesthetic. The danger is always implicit in New Criticism that by selecting any passage and then offering an analysis of it, you are, by definition, re-distributing the reality of effect, the balance of harmony when reading.

Hirsch's view has been recapitulated by other formalist critics who have disagreed with Leavis. Geoffrey Johnson Sadok argues that 'the quiet victory of disinterested goodness which Leavis credits Sissy with is perhaps the most continued and embarrassing incident in *Hard Times*.' But more importantly, the weight given to the circus's vitality and to the moral goodness of Sissy, is too great for them to bear against the massive evils of the society; and more interestingly, he notes Leavis's failure to see how Christian Dickens's novel is in tone and spirit. In between these two essays, comes John Gibson, who also finds the symbolic role allocated to circus and characters insufficient and thinks Leavis's apology for disinterested goodness insufficient for the 'unhappy shambles of Dickens's art', in a novel whose method he finds 'pallid, dispassionate, slow and uncomplex.' (*Gibson*, 1965, p. 95) These critics seem determined to outdo one another in providing disapproving adjectives for the novel.

Nice work

A much more restrained response to Leavis is that of David Lodge in his *Language of Fiction* (1966). Lodge, at the time of writing, could be characterised as a New Critic, though as the years have gone by he has tended to bend with the wind. He has also participated in recent theoretical debates, though with a certain agnosticism and provincial caution. But, as this essay demonstrates, his interest always lay in language, and he might claim, quite reasonably, that he has not changed, but that the times have moved on.

Like Hirsch and Leavis, he has to rely on the method of choosing selected passages, and looking for patterns of repetition and style. In essence, Lodge finds Dickens's rhetoric insufficient for what needs to be said. 'Dickens could only offer a disembodied and vaguely defined benevolence as a cure for the ills of Coketown because he had rejected all the alternatives.' (*Lodge*, p. 146) Thus the novel is only partially persuasive because Dickens's rhetoric is only partially adequate to the tasks he set himself. Given the subjects of *Hard Times*, industrialism, education, utilitarianism, these beg, in a way, a certain type of evidence, so that if a novel does not rely on statistical enquiry, commissions, reports acted on by Parliamentary legislation, but on a generalised 'fancy', then, it is argued, it requires a very powerful rhetoric to overcome its sociological deficiencies. If it fails to possess that power, no amount of statistical material will save it, but the lack of such information 'will almost certainly damn it.' Lodge keeps apart sociology and literature, reserving a place for the powerful rhetoric, but in this novel he finds it absent, so he finds Leavis's judgement overblown, and *Hard Times* not a good novel of its self-appointed type. As a 'fable', it is not fabulous enough in its language. And although an essay which does actually examine Dickens's rhetoric, its aim is still to come to a value judgement.

The historical approach: another Cambridge don

Leavis's grand pronouncements were also confronted by a quite different sort of approach, those of the literary historian. John

Holloway, building upon the work of K. J. Fielding and Phillip Collins, both doyens of Dickens scholarship, whilst acknowledging the New Critical doctrine that proof of value 'can come only from the text', nevertheless, seeks to re-situate *Hard Times* in its contemporary historical setting. Reasonably enough, if this is a satire, then it seems a way of discovering if it was an effective one, by looking at what Dickens's objects of attack actually were. To make the distinctiveness of approach clear, the idealist or formal critic tends to follow Matthew Arnold's famous prescription for criticism, 'to see the object as in itself it really is'; the historical critic counters with to see the object it really *was*.

The formalist critic evacuates history from his account; the literary historian believes that meaning must be tempered by a historical knowledge. Since, at the moment, there is a considerable debate surrounding what constitutes historical knowledge, and, indeed, whether we can ever know the past except through the filter of the contemporary, literary history here means something quite empirical. It might raise such questions as: were there schools really like Gradgrind's? Was the curriculum that narrow and enforcing? What was the true state of the trades union movement when Dickens satirised it? Was Dickens's knowledge of the unions based upon his visit to the Preston Strike in January, 1854? In other words, an historical approach will tend to look for the raw materials which are transformed into a novel and to which the novel stands as either typical or atypical, representational or distortive. Evidence, as in biographical approaches or the textual approach may, of course, be drawn from any sources available.

Holloway cites, for instance, as extra-textual evidence, Dickens's speeches at the time of the composition of *Hard Times*, at a civic dinner at Birmingham, in which the author praises industry in terms, allowing for exaggeration, which would not have displeased Bounderby. Or, again Dickens can write of Lancashire mills as: 'the factory itself is certainly not a "thing of beauty" in its externals, but it is a grand machine in its organisation – the men, the fingers, and the iron and steel, all work together for one common end.' (*Holloway*, p. 166) This sort of evidence (there is more which Holloway brings forward) leads him to conclude that in terms of the industrial degradation that the book projects, Dickens, for all his opposition to the 'hard fact men' actually subscribes to the idea of an identity of interest between men and masters.

Holloway withholds from Dickens the praise which Leavis

accords him, claiming that Dickens was not a profound and prophetic genius with insight into the deepest levels of human experience. Vigorous and good hearted, he may be, but, ultimately 'shallow'. Holloway demonstrates Dickens's lack of profound insight by drawing attention to the schoolroom scene (one which Leavis had specially praised) so as to reinforce his insistent proposal that Dickens is essentially a middle-class philistine, and that the satire of taste shows that to be so, and is further evidence of his lack of profundity.

Carpets and wallpaper

The issue, for Holloway, is specifically locatable in Chapter 2, in the interrogations which follow the definition of a horse. The Government gentleman asks the children: 'would you paper a room with representations of horses?' [p. 51]. The same question is asked of carpets a little later. The historical approach has to discover what the actual contemporary debate was about before one can know on what side Dickens was. Where, then, does the author stand? For this we need to know what Dickens is satirising.

K. J. Fielding believes that the vital clue to this satirical episode lies in Dickens's manuscript plan for Chapter 2, which reads, 'Marlborough House. *Cole.*' Marlborough House was the headquarters of the Department of Practical Art, part of the Board of Trade, which had been set up in the wake of The Great Exhibition of 1851 (which, incidentally, Dickens loathed) to foster good modern design in industry. Henry Cole, an acquaintance of Dickens, and Secretary of the Department of Science and Art from 1853 to 1873, was one of its prime movers. But what was good 'modern' design in mid-Victorian England? Holloway believes that the group of which Cole was a leading member is not to be identified with a 'crude and vulgar photographic realism ... Bounderby art' (*Holloway*, p. 164), but, rather, that they are to be seen as opposing the heavily floral, over-elaborated, uselessly ornate art which found its way into everything. They desired a new functionalism and a more moderate, indeed 'practical' sort of art. Thus to satirise Cole is to defend what he opposes, and this, Holloway argues, is what Dickens is doing when he shows the Government gentleman lecturing Sissy on what is good taste, informing her where it is to come from: 'We hope to have, before long, a board of fact, composed of commissioners of fact, who will force the people to be a people of fact, and of nothing but fact.' [p. 52]

Cole's views on art and design are thus identified with utilitarianism and bureaucracy, and thus to be damned. However, as Fielding
points out, it is highly unlikely that a representative from the Board
of Trade would be talking to schoolchildren in Lancashire. Marlborough House had no connection with schools, and it is highly
improbable that children would have been given lessons on aesthe-
tics. Dickens is here, on the one hand, indulging in a private joke
against a contemporary, and, on the other, he is taking a tendency
and magnifying it in his satire, and mixing up fact and fiction for his
own didactic purposes. Phillip Collins thinks Dickens was lucky to
get away with the private joke (since no one seems to have noticed),
but this personal ragging makes sense within the larger critique in
terms of the overall imagery. The details of horses and flowers (both
traditional emblems of the natural world) are repeated later in the
novel. Gradgrind tumbles about annihilating the flowers of existence, Tom destroys flowers in the rose garden, Bitzer is kept at bay
by an advancing horse. Collins, like Fielding, believes the episode
vis-à-vis Marlborough House is inaccurate, but it does 'express a
spirit active in some of the schools of that time and place.' (*Collins,
Dickens and Education*, p. 158)

Holloway is less prepared to let things go as being 'the spirit of the
time.' If Dickens is so critical of the functional corrective to
Victorian florid excess, then he is complicit with the philistines, the
reactionaries of his age who would maintain those tasteless designs.
He is not of the modern party, and, by implication, the Utilitarians
are.

The difficulty of seeing, exactly, where Dickens stood is somewhat
complicated by the fact that history has gone against Dickens,
though what he criticises is remarkably proleptic, even in 1854, of
what was to actually happen to the whirls and swirls of the floral and
the ornate as Victorian design was comprehensively swept away by
modernist (twentieth-century) ideas of art and design.

'You must use,' said the gentleman, 'for all these purposes,
combinations and modifications (in primary colours) of mathematical figures which are susceptible of proof and demonstration.'
[p. 52]

Given the simplification necessary, this could be a recipe for
Bauhaus design, and everything which flowed from it; think, for
example, of the bright colours and geometric designs of Art Deco.

Holloway, therefore, cannot resist showing Dickens on the side of the unenlightened, and thus provides further damning evidence of how Dickens misunderstands utilitarianism. But one can argue that what Dickens is doing with this art criticism is showing, as he shows with other aspects of society, what happens when an informing idea is carried to excess, and then it becomes dehumanising, perhaps farcically so, and ultimately denaturing.

To broaden out Holloway's purpose, what he is doing is showing Dickens as part of a contemporary cultural debate, and he is showing him to be clearly on one side of it. He believes that Dickens's satirical treatment of utilitarianism as a serious, if some-what diffuse philosophy of life, is wholly misjudged, and that his satire of it, shows in his inability to fully comprehend it.

This detailed historicising of the text may seem to some to be beside the point. After all, what Dickens is satirising is plain enough, the demented thoroughness of those committed to a single dogma or doctrine, whether it applies to what people should have on their walls or what they should read, or what they should study at school. It is all of a piece throughout. Once obsessed by an idea (any idea), society becomes deformed. Yet, even granted that larger purpose, there is still a reckoning to be made with what the object of the satire is. Holloway's historical approach sets out to achieve two things. Firstly, it wants to rescue *Hard Times* for history and thus to dispossess the Leavisite excessive praise; and, secondly, it wants to rescue utilitarianism from Dickens's savaging of it.

Here then, is an historical approach which is a useful corrective, and one which often exercises the critic, which is that the historical meaning of the text to the contemporary reader (even if they miss the joke about Cole, they would have understood the complaints about facts and liberal economics) is part of an intellectual and social context located in a definite historical era. One of the complaints raised against such historical reconstruction is that it says nothing about the value of the novel (Holloway concedes this), nor, and this is much more important, does it make clear what a novel is meant to mean or how it should be read by non-contemporary readers for whom the history, and especially the history of competing ideas, has been superseded by other ideas.

By drawing attention to the specificity of contemporary reference the historical approach can, however, create as many problems as it can solve. For, if carried to its logical extreme, then it would mean that it is never possible to read an older text and understand it within the historical knowledge which informed it at the time of its writing. The reductio ad absurdum of this notion would be that no one could read anything at all without re-creating the entire historical knowledge necessary for its interpretation. As we have seen with just one minor detail, the Department of Practical Art, and the schoolroom, this is often a lengthy and complex business, and history does not conveniently stop at any one point and say, this is necessary to read the text, and this is not. In fact, what happens with this sort of historical approach is that lines are drawn, and only so much of what is thought necessary is brought forward as evidence. It should be recognised that this truncation is arbitrary. It is only common sense and common experience of reading that prevents the background from totally overwhelming the text and making it impossible to read at all.

Theoretical approaches: deconstruction; now, what I want, is theory

Whether texts are 'readable' at all is also one of the persistent questions which bothers theoretical, especially so called post-structuralist approaches, to the text. Deconstruction, as the most radical of the strategies for dealing with texts, asks searching questions of just about every assumption we usually make, for it is, in essence, a radically sceptical philosophy; within it nothing is certain any more. Deconstruction is not 'summarisable', for its central tenet is that it is a process of working with a text (which need not be a realist novel or a lyric poem), and it demonstrates its approach by its intimate engagement with language.

Steven Connor's deconstructionist reading of *Hard Times* (*Connor*, 1985) is a good example of what deconstruction actually does; with a little help from a primer on deconstruction, and by carefully following his graduated series of different theoretical readings of selected Dickens novels, it might be possible for the initiated to follow his arguments. However, it is not a familiar way of thinking (at least not outside the hermetic cells of university literary criticism), and its assumptions and premises are wholly antagonistic to those which have underlain all the critical approaches so far. Underlying the critical approaches we have looked at is, ultimately, a view which is concerned with unity where criticism is concerned to reveal a unifying idea by showing how a text is organically related.

Apparent incoherence is really coherence. Deconstruction begins from the opposite pole to this and tries to show how a unified single meaning is impossible. Texts, because they are made up of language, which is an endless system of signs and signifiers which are always relational to other signs and signifiers, are really full of incoherences, indecisions, ambiguities, hesitations, indeterminacies. Deconstructionist readings, therefore, nearly always privilege incoherence at the expense of coherence. Connor is aware of this, and warns of it becoming the new orthodoxy, and also adds the almost obligatory critical health warning with which all deconstructionists caption their readings so as to warn the unbelieving readers; 'all this does not mean a license to mash any text up into a dog's breakfast, about which one can say more or less what they like.' (*Connor*, p. 90)

No one, alas, has yet come up with a good way of preventing these canine meals being readily available. Using the concepts of 'metaphor' and 'metonomy' what, in a nutshell, Connor advances, is the argument (and many deconstructionist readings attempt to discover the same thing) that although, ostensibly, *Hard Times* has a clear object in view, which is to show the opposition of fact and fancy in which the author declares his preference for the one against the other, what actually happens at the textual, linguistic level is that these oppositions cannot be consistently sustained, and they begin to lose their distinction from one another; and thus, the text 'fights against itself' in creating a meaning and intelligibility. Even with what is thought to be so clearly a text which maintains the difference of fact and fancy, this is not really so. Hence the text is not a coherent one at all; earlier critics have merely made it so. Hence, our:

> firm convictions of the clarity of its structure actually require the suspension of awareness of certain rather important internal inconsistencies. These inconsistencies have a residual force though working athwart the main narrative, but also, in a peculiar way, sustaining it. (*Connor*, p. 105)

To make sense of this, it is necessary, firstly, to acknowledge that deconstruction derives one basic tenet from psycho-analysis, which is that primary distinction between the hidden and the revealed, familiar to everyone as the 'conscious' and the 'sub-conscious', to use the Freudian terms. Connor concludes his intricate linguistic analysis by pointing out:

Because the book is so committed to the projection of the stark opposites of Fact and Fancy, the risk is all the greater of discovering it to be haunted by internal difference, of the book being revealed as another text entirely from the one it represents itself to be. Nonetheless, this is the dangerous story that *Hard Times* begins to tell about itself. (*Connor*, p. 106)

A deconstructive example: Mrs Sparsit's staircase

Mrs Sparsit, as a character in the novel *Hard Times*, is granted a metaphor by the narrator of the novel:

Now, Mrs Sparsit was not a poetical woman; but she took an idea, in the nature of an allegorical fancy, into her head .... She erected in her mind a mighty Staircase, with a dark pit of shame and ruin at the bottom; and down those stairs, from day to day and hour to hour, she saw Louisa coming. [pp. 226–7]

The chapter in which we are told of Mrs Sparsit's entry into poetic fancy is called 'Mrs Sparsit's Staircase'. The two subsequent chapters are called 'Lower and Lower', and 'Down'. What Connor here draws attention to is the way in which Mrs Sparsit's obsession with this metaphor is so highly melodramatic; indeed there is something satisfyingly appropriate about Mrs Sparsit's unconscious choice of this debased literary mode to embody her spite and it reveals, as he puts it:

the unconscious complicity between Dickens's language and Mrs. Sparsit's is a sign of a more deeply rooted association between the dominant metaphorical mode of signification it condemns in Gradgrind and the party of Fact ... Metaphor is repeatedly used to discredit metaphor as Dickens mounts a systematic assault on systematic thought. (*Connor*, pp. 99–100)

What Connor calls 'unconscious complicity' has, of course, been noticed before. Butt and Tillotson refer to the strange way in which the author gives a character a metaphor (it is Mrs Sparsit's idea, not the narrator's idea, though he must know about it). According to their reading, which was functional and editorial, Dickens had a structural problem in trying to show how Louisa's 'descent', in other words, a gradual change in consciousness, 'is to be brought home to the readers.' Shortage of space made any sort of development difficult and therefore the staircase image is used as a sort of shorthand sign for representing that development. But they make no comment on the curious nature, as it appears to the deconstructionist reading, of this identification of character and author. Surely, authors' or author-narrators' thoughts, to be more exact, are not to be confused with characters' thoughts, and should be separated.

For Butt and Tillotson, it is an insignificant confusion; indeed, they refer to the point almost apologetically. Dickens's space problem leads to bad management. But to the deconstructionist reading, this is a point deep in signification. Connor argues that the ironic distance between author and character is abandoned, and that the complicity is to see Dickens's control of metaphor as no less coercive than Mrs Sparsit's. But, since the theme of the book as a whole is the way in which metaphors are used for control and manipulation, then the appeal to fancy is here undermined.

Now, clearly, something odd is going on. A character in a novel is credited with having an idea, a flight of fancy, then Dickens (the narrator) steals the idea back, and uses it. Mrs Sparsit cannot write the novel in which she is a character: only Dickens can do that. Is this woman taking over? Is Dickens failing to control his character, or is he really desirous of the 'complicity' Connor accuses him of? Is this 'lapse', this 'mistake' a sign of an unconscious wish on the part of the author to be *like* Mrs Sparsit, and thus to undermine the very idea of fairy tale, which is meant to be the positive in the novel against the sheer world of Fact. Later, Connor speculates interestingly about the relationship of author to his creations, and sees generally a desire for control on the author's part which belies a terrible anxiety for the control of meaning. Dickens's public readings, for instance, are used as evidence of Dickens's desire to maintain his own presence in his writings, whereas, as we know, all writings, once they have left the author, can be read in a multiplicity of ways by a variety of readers. A stage performance limits the literal 'reading' to one reader. (Of course, even despite the greater manipulative potential of the dramatic rendition over the private reading, no audience is controllable either.)

How significant is Dickens's 'mistake' in confusing narrator or author-narrator and character? The pragmatic view is, simply, that it is a lapse, but that there were good empirical reasons why it occurred. To the deconstructionist approach, however, such a lapse is always crucial. As on the psycho-analytical couch, every verbal detail has significance, and no detail is any more important or trivial than any other detail, unless the interpreter, or reader, finds it so. As another example, Connor analyses Sissy's confusion of 'statistics' and 'stutterings' (verbal confusions, sometimes inaccurately called Freudian slips) when she is explaining her performance at school to Louisa:

> 'Then Mr. M'Choakumchild said he would try me once more. And he said, Here are the stutterings – '
> 'Statistics,' said Louisa.
> 'Yes, Miss Louisa – they always remind me of stutterings and that's another of my mistakes.' [p. 97]

Apologising for the tediousness, Connor then proceeds to offer a two page analysis (complete with diagrams) of this joke, the conclusion of which is that the stutter is an instability of meaning in the text which is incompatible with the supposedly authoritative meaning of the narration.

Deconstructionist approaches to a text are, by definition, almost endless. They are inconclusive, and generally generating of other deconstructionist readings, and the process is such that my reading of Connor can be deconstructed by the reader of this book, and so on, *ad infinitum* . . . It depends which details one chooses to isolate and use. Connor not only uses Mrs Sparsit's staircase and Louisa's stutterings, but also Gradgrind's language, and Bounderby's fancies. But there are all the things which he does not consider at such detailed length of exposition, which, therefore, in the deconstructionist approach, represent a 'repression' (another borrowing from psycho-analysis).

But of course, what the critic does to a text, another critic can do to that reading of the text. Connor's argument about stutterings and statistics, which he shows to be an unstable point of meaning, he summarises in the following categories:

> The reader therefore flickers between the two readings, the adult and the childish, the meaningful and the meaningless.

Now, this language is ripe for deconstruction. Leaving aside the question of which 'reader' (Connor?, any deconstructionist?, any other reader, etc.), and why not just say I, except that to say 'the reader' is to gain an authority which the 'I' doesn't have. And, readers do not 'flicker'. Lights flicker, and so, by extension as they are the conduits of light to the brain or consciousness, eyes flicker, in the act of reading. Of course, this is an analogy, a metaphor in which things stand for one another, especially that called synecdoche, in which, as Dickens's use of 'hands' for factory operatives, the part stands for the whole, or, as here, the whole stands for the part.

A non-deconstructionist reader would simply say this is inexact English, but we know what the author means: the eyes = the reader, and his poor expression is not worth bothering about. The deconstructionist approach, because every detail is capable of significant interpretation, would query his metaphor and see in it the critic's anthropomorphising of language. Earlier, as we (you and I, reader) have seen the text 'connives' in what it condemns with Mrs Sparsit's staircase. Can a text 'connive'? Does this not imply human will and intention, and is not intention a profound fallacy of the deconstructionist critic? Is Connor's own rhetoric, then, for all its stated adherence to theory, remarkably personalising, indeed, over-humanising in its metaphors? Does this say, therefore, that he is not really happy with this theoretical rhetoric, though he commits himself to its discourse? Is his text, as Dickens's text, really athwart itself? And in particular, is he really at ease using the term 'Dickens', despite the problematic notion that there is an author at all? A deconstructionist approach, or, as its practitioners prefer to say, 'reading', can bring before us certain inescapable properties of language. It can, and usually does, demonstrate how mistaken we are if we think that any text reveals to the interpreter one and one meaning alone, and it can alert us to details that formerly might have received little or no attention, but which examined, allow us to unravel all sorts of contradictions in the text. But to be conducted properly, it requires a primary knowledge and understanding of the literary criticism which has preceded it, it needs a more than scanty acquaintance with whole areas of social and philosophical thought, and it often needs to be carried out at woefully excessive length. Above all, it is a demonstrative process of logical expositional analysis. It is noteworthy that much of it is lugubriously long-winded, something which Connor's account of Hard Times mercifully avoids.

Part Two: Appraisal

By now it should be becoming clear what sort of critical comment *Hard Times* has elicited from its critics. Varied as they have been in their approaches, essentially their responses have been evaluative ones. Its admirers, Ruskin, Shaw, Leavis, Craig, have been willing to make a case for it by pleading tolerance for its faults. Its sociologically-minded detractors have evaluated the novel in ways which discover it failing to meet the criteria of what an analysis of industrial society should do; in particular, they admonished its failure to adequately convey an authentic sense of working-class life, or industrialism, or the trades union movement.

On the other hand, essentially apolitical critics such as Lodge or Hirsch see the failure in its inability to convince as a fable because its form and language are insufficiently powerful for what it purportedly is trying to combat. They have sought in it a defence of the imagination (Fancy) which the novel supposedly endorses, but suggest that what is offered by way of symbol and myth, is weak and ineffective. Paradoxically, a work of fiction which should be a demonstration of the value of fable is actually weaker than Dickens's other novels, which in their largeness of scope and breadth of vision create what this novel can only inadequately state as desirable. Most important of all, the circus, interesting as it may be as a quasi-anarchic counterpoint to the rigidities of the 'hard fact' school fails utterly as a symbol for the upholding of serious artistic values.

Mixed in with these debates has been the almost universal reproach (Leavis the notable exception) that *Hard Times* is the least representative of Dickens's great gifts and qualities as a novelist. His vivid characterisation, his intricate plotting (*Hard Times* has the simplest of all of his plots, and carefully avoids his fond liking for the device of inheritance), his magnificent, if sometimes over-elaborate powers of description, his penetrating wit, and, largest disappointment of all, his tremendous capacity for literary humour – all these

ng. Dickens needs the broad canvas with a
cast of interconnected characters. He is not Jane
our families in a country village is the very thing
n the epic writer is reduced to the miniaturist,
Dickens needs length for his imaginative vision and
rd Times defeats him.

oint there are those who see the Hard Times versus
othe   work discussion as a futile comparison. Monroe
Engel (1959) argued that:

> it is silly to prolong the arbitrary see-saw between Hard Times and
> the rest of Dickens's work. It is more to the point to see that the
> greatest virtues of Hard Times are Dickens's characteristic virtues,
> but less richly present in this book than in many others.

Inevitably, such a comparison will be drawn. The Leavisite
exception of the book as 'masterpiece' has magnified the difference,
thus inviting the contrast. But Engel is probably right. Criticism can
more positively attend to what the novel is rather than how good it
is.

What is Hard Times?

The first thing to do is to circumnavigate Leavis's characterisation
of the novel as moral fable. Ever since Leavis coined the term critics
have been constrained by using it. Perhaps it is time to abandon it
altogether and in its place offer a definition which will orientate
criticism in different directions. Several critics have in fact tried to
do this and substituted a variety of terms; 'romance', 'satire',
'romantic drama', 'parable', 'morality drama', 'dramatic comedy'.
These definitional terms are not, it needs to be said, absolute or
exclusive distinctions. Rather, they are indexical emphases, each
one useful in its own way, each one opening up certain perceptions.
The purpose in each instance is an enabling one (as, indeed, was
Leavis's formulation).

What is for me unsatisfactory about moral fable is that it did not
linger on the characteristics of fables. Apart from pointing to the
symbolic value of Sissy or the circus as the benign upholders of the
spontaneous imagination in a relentlessly utilitarian world, the
category was very much left undeveloped. This might be because

there is very little to say. Fable, if it means anything at all, implies the fabulous, but there is little that can approach that quality in *Hard Times*. There are no surprising coincidences or wonderful revelations or brilliant reversals. The discovery that Mrs Pegler is Bounderby's jettisoned mother comes as no great shock. Nor is there any masterful triumph of good over evil. Tom's escape from Bounderby's clutches is a temporary respite and a temporary victory for the circus folk. Sissy and Bitzer at the novel's close are as irreconcilably opposed as they were at the beginning when the sun shone on them both. Gradgrind's change of heart and degradation into a broken 'white-haired decrepit man' does not come about by any magic conversion, but by the tragic misery of his daughter into which recognition he has to be forcibly shocked, and by the pathetic spectacle of seeing his son as a common criminal.

Nor are there any magical settings which can make a Dickens novel so surreal. The description of Coketown with its 'melancholy madness', elephants and fairy lights, although it may border on the phantasmagoric, is, like calling Gradgrind an 'ogre', more whimsey than sustained fabulousness. And the dismal life of Stephen Blackpool is the very converse of the fable. Instead of fable I would proffer as the most capacious alternative the term 'dramatic satire'. For the remainder of this appraisal I shall elaborate on how weight may be given to both terms. My first stress falls on aspects of the dramatising quality of Dickens's imagination.

Dickens the dramatiser

Dickens, it hardly needs repeating, is probably the most dramatic of all English novelists. He himself believed that 'every good writer of fiction, though he may not adopt the dramatic form, writes in effect for the stage.' Dramatic has two meanings here. There is first the sense of drama as oppositional conflict in which the reader/audience participate in the force and counterforce of argument and character in such a way which allows for sympathy and recoil. And there is the other meaning which is that of heightened effect which can result in the theatrical and melodramatic, hence Ruskin's acute diagnosis of the 'circle of stage fire'.

It was a nineteenth-century critic, E. P. Whipple (1877), who, in a mixed review of the novel, located its major flaw in what he saw as the confused mixture of the dramatic and the satiric. He conceded that Dickens's creation of character was as a humorous satirist of flagrant abuses, but he felt that drama demands of its creator a certain sympathy from its author, and that Dickens abandons that sympathy when he allows his satire to take over. Bounderby is a good example of what happens when the creator of dramatic fiction becomes confused about these rules of separation. Whipple's argument does contain an underlying sense of realism in the creation of character it is true, but he felt that Dickens should leave the 'cheering views of the amelioration of the condition of the race to come down from those hard thinkers whose benevolent impulses push them to the investigation of neutral and economic laws.' (*Ford and Monod*, p. 326) In other words, Whipple diagnosed that the dramatic and the satiric, the latter often identified with the insistent voice of the narrator, could produce a sort of disjunction. What Whipple believed to be amiss, I believe, makes *Hard Times* interesting; the dramatic and the satire combined give it its distinctive quality.

Relations between dramatic and satiric

Clearly, what Whipple did not admire was Dickens's adoption of mixed modes of writing within a novel, even though he writes in a singular voice. The novel does move uneasily between different rhetorical modes. The narrator's ironical animadversions, for instance, are often troublesome, particularly if one is sympathetic to the targets of the satire, in that they are aimed at large diffuse enemies. They are very generalised too. Take his comment on the social reformers arguing amongst themselves as to the best way to bring about social improvement, but reduced by Dickens to:

> portentious infants . . . scratched one another's faces and pulled one another's hair . . . Body number one, said they must take everything on trust. Body number two, said they must take everything on political economy. Body number three, wrote leaden little books for them, showing how the good grown-up baby invariably got to the Savings-bank, and the bad grown-up baby invariably got transported. [p. 90]

On its own terms this works well enough as contemporary satire, but it consorts oddly with, say, the scene of Sissy's reconciliation with Louisa, and Louisa's with her father (Book 3, Chapter 1), which is a blending of the realistic and the pathetic, but a dramatic moment in the narrative which is an integral part of the plot.

Satirical sideswipes at social reformers and improvers, a role none of the characters is meant to perform, may be rhetorical flourishes, but are not relevant to the rest of the book. Lawrence Lerner (1978) has remarked that with Dickens, style and content can often be locked in splendid opposition, and that so far from being depressed by what he sees, Dickens is 'exhilarated by the metaphoric opportunities it offers'. (*Lerner*, p. 207) True or not, the authorial commentary is of a different order of writing than the dramatic set pieces. They are related because Dickens makes them so, but this often by force of juxtaposition than by a natural artistic integrity. But even if one puts to one side the many places in the novel where the narrator takes a strong hand and uses the mode of direct address to make his pronouncements on themes and social ills, it is still possible to see that even within the dramatic moments themselves, satire is still actively at play. Indeed, throughout (hence Whipple's and others' displeasure), the satiric is informed by the dramatic from the 'effects', to use Dickens's own word. One need only look at the first description of Bounderby:

> He was a rich man: broker, merchant, manufacturer, and what not. A big, loud man, with a stare and a metallic laugh. A man made out of a coarse material, which seemed to have been stretched to make so much of him. A man with a great puffed head and forehead, swelled veins in his temples, and such a strained skin to his face that it seemed to hold his eyes open and lift his eyebrows up. A man with a pervading appearance on him of being inflated like a balloon, and ready to start ... A man who was always proclaiming through that brassy speaking-trumpet of a voice of his, his old ignorance and his old poverty. A man who was the Bully of humility. [p. 58]

That voice will, of course, terrify (in the same chapter) the ineffectual Mrs Gradgrind, and will bully and try to terrify Stephen and Louisa. The self-inflation of the self-made man will be a recurrent motif, with the metaphor of swelling and physical self-magnification used to mimic the psychological self-aggrandisement. But this highly coloured description, which sets out the hardness of Bounderby's character outside of which he is not going to move, and which Dickens will amplify and elaborate upon in several ways, contains a single, seemingly unimportant comment which moves the character description from dramatic to satiric. It is the 'and what not'. It is a dismissal of what has preceded it. Brokers, merchants and manufacturers are, of course, the pillars of the mercantile utilitarian industry. But these positions in society, says the narrator, are no more than a 'what not'. Admittedly, the detail is a tiny one, but makes its effect nonetheless. The Captains of Industry are reducible to an afterthought, as it were.

The dramatic scene

But there is another way in which Dickens is so manifestly a dramatic writer. This is not in his colourful ways of describing character, or in his highly stylised dialogue, but in his use of the theatrical, where he translates the representation of theatre into novelistic form. Two types stand out in particular. One is the device of the crowded scene (a mode used in many of his novels, and often brilliantly illuminated by his illustrators, especially Phiz). Examples in this novel include the opening scene in the schoolroom, Slackbridge's farcical oration, and the chapter in Book 3 entitled 'Philosophical'. But the most dramatic example is in 'Found' (Chapter 5) in which Bounderby is confronted by Mrs Sparsit and his mother. A character within the novel appears to other characters, as well as to the readers, like an actor upon a stage in front of whom he is made to act out a performance. Here, the spectators come in from the street led by the spiteful avenging Mrs Sparsit:

> Accordingly, the chance witnesses on the ground, consisting of the busiest of the neighbours to the number of some five-and-twenty, closed in after Sissy and Rachael; as they closed in after Mrs Sparsit and her prize; and the whole body made a disorderly irruption into Mr Bounderby's dining-room, where the people behind lost not a moment's time in mounting on the chairs, to get the better of the people in front. [p. 278]

Bounderby's dining room becomes a public entertainment. As we follow the comical scene through to its culmination in which the bully of humility is himself humbled ('shorn and forlorn' [p. 281]) we realise that Dickens is using one of his established metaphors for dramatic theatre, which is the law court. In reality, this scene becomes a mock trial. The 'chance witnesses' later become the spectators, and then the bystanders of the trial. There are accusations, a star witness (Mrs Pegler brought forward), devastating evidence, and the language of the law court. What we learn is that Bounderby was not brought up in the gutter, nor was he uneducated, but that he was kept by the hard work of his mother in a village shop so that the trial of Mrs Pegler by an odd metamorphosis becomes the trial of Bounderby, who is, of course, Mrs Sparsit's real target. Mrs Sparsit, with obvious delight, plays the part of all the law court officers. 'Fetch Mr Bounderby down!' is mock courtroom style, an injunction which is repeated. This then becomes a form of theatrical entertainment conducted in humorous terms; and of course the villain is unmasked in his hypocrisy which the casual bystanders of Coketown relish as entertainment. (It is more interesting than the circus, one has to admit.) The scene is brilliantly realised in brief strokes, the bystanders murmuring in sympathy as Bounderby walks up and down getting redder and redder, and 'swelling larger and larger', Dickens's main metaphor for his self-inflated importance.

The theatrical device

Another popular theatrical device common in the theatre (especially Shakespeare and Renaissance drama), is the eavesdropping scene, here used in Chapter 11 (Book the Second) in which Mrs Sparsit with her Coriolanian nose interferes in Louisa's life as well as in Mrs Pegler's. In a novel, in which information can be conveyed directly from narrator to reader this can appear awkward, but it is essential for the plot that Mrs Sparsit overhears the cause of Louisa's unhappiness which is her growing fondness for Harthouse which will eventually lead to her breakdown.

Dickens was a master of the pursuit scene, and the eavesdropping is part of the narrative thrust which takes in Mrs Sparsit waiting at the station, twigging that Louisa and Harthouse are meeting secretly, following, overhearing, following again at the station. In a novel an eavesdropping scene might appear an old-fashioned and quaint convention, and in a way it is. But it serves as an example of greater narrative complexity and unity, for it brings together not only the illicit lovers, but inserts Mrs Sparsit into their story, and connects up characters and their lives in a way that narrative exposition would keep apart. In other words, as with the mock trial scene at which Sissy and Rachael are also present, it is Dickens's way of connecting, a way of perceiving that his unsympathetic readers often denigrate as forced coincidence, but which his admirers call a unifying vision. Yet, the theatrical device is part of something greater, which is Dickens at full narrative stretch in his most economical mode. Think of Dickens's long descriptions of railways, then notice how here he has to settle for the most impressionistic touch:

> The seizure of the station with a fit of trembling, gradually deepening to a complaint of the heart, announced the train. Fire and steam, and smoke, and red light; a hiss, a crash, a bell, and a shriek; Louisa put into one carriage, Mrs Sparsit put into another: the little station a desert speck in the thunder-storm. [p. 237]

This is the sort of narrative novel writing which a critic such as Whipple, who at one point invokes Jonsonian satire (a comparison which Leavis also made) would not be offended by. What he objects to is Dickens's use of the non-dramatic modes, such as in his direct narratorial address to the readers, often used as indicative commentary on his characters and their actions, and, of course, in his characterising of the ideas which inform Gradgrind's and Bounderby's behaviour. Dickens can casually use the throw-away line which so infuriated Martineau ('chopping people up with their machinery' [p. 145]), but this exaggerated effect is not isolated, it is part of the total way of seeing. If the dramatic is satirised, then the satiric is dramatised.

Nor is this combination of drama and satire arbitrary. It is necessary for what Dickens has to say. Fielding put his finger on the problem when he remarked that:

> the novel has such a broad purpose, even though it included references to some of Dickens's living contemporaries which most of them were unable to recognise, and satire of specific abuses which were too pointed to be understood by the general reader, and it is only by understanding this broader purpose . . . that one can see how it unifies Dickens's remarks on Stephen Blackpool's marriage, the aesthetic problems of the third gentleman, the theft from the bank . . . A careful reading shows that he succeeded in giving them a unified coherence and power. (*Fielding*, p. 162)

The problem for articulated criticism, but not for attentive readers is to find the description which will summarise and identify this broader purpose without it becoming just a list of satires, or disconnected themes. But it is true, I feel, that the more one reads *Hard Times*, the more relationships, such as the one Fielding cites, begin to appear. This is a common experience with reading, but only provable with greater concentration. Much of this takes place at the textual or linguistic level, rather than in the more general or thematic categorisations. Fielding's list is extendable in many directions. One could as well ask, what have Sissy's flowers on the wall got to do with Bitzer's partaking of chop and sherry, or, Bounderby's self-dramatising bluster with Gradgrind's educational system, Mrs Pegler with Tom Gradgrind? The point is there are many relationships in the novel, not all of them of the same kind. Some are social, some are thematic, some linked by plot, some linked by language; but the unifying is endless.

The broad purpose

One of the first and easiest things to say about *Hard Times* because it is a truism, would be that the novel is a bitter attack on materialism. Dickens thus belongs to that community of romantic protest which enlisted so many nineteenth-century poets and novelists. But this is insufficient unless we make clear what materialism means in this context. Materialism is a big word; it means several things. What Dickens is attacking is not so much the material products of the deforming organisation of society (although we have Coketown's purple pollution, its monotony, its industrial injury) but what it is which informs all materialist thinking and behaviour. He perceives materialism for what it often pretends not to be, which is a particular abstract state of mind. Here it is identified, possibly distortedly, with utilitarianism, often called Benthamism, after its founder Jeremy Bentham, the legal reformer and a philosopher associated with a particular set of economic proposals ultimately derived from Adam Smith, and resulting, when augmented by assorted social views of human behaviour, in a totalising and schematised perception of society. But materialism, as the novel acknowledges is a protean monster.

> And what you couldn't state in figures, or show to be purchaseable in the cheapest market and saleable in the dearest, was not, and never should be, world without end, Amen. [p. 66]

Dickens, invoking the biblical language, comments bitterly, not only on *laissez-faire* economics, but also on what is reducible to a convenient formula. For, what Bounderby, Gradgrind, Harthouse and Bitzer endorse by their actions and their individual rhetorics is not only the reduction of utilitarianism, but the abstraction upon which that philosophy is supported. Abstractions have to be given embodiment in language and in images. What Dickens wanted to show, in his various examples, was the overwhelming force of the sociologically-driven mind when it becomes the sole way of seeing the world, and the only way in which reality is to be talked about. This is to stress the novel as a social novel and as an historical document, a ruthless indictment of a ruthless society which so enraged pompous Victorians and has so disappointed twentieth-century politically motivated critics. Once, however, we acknowledge that abstraction itself underlines this focus of attack, we can see that the satire is as much a literary satire, as it is a social and a political one; it is as much concerned with language as it is with political systems.

In this section I shall approach the novel from a different angle altogether and consider *Hard Times* as a novel about writing because Dickens as social critic and Dickens as writer are so inextricably interconnected. To prevent that angle being too oblique, it is necessary to say what I mean by 'writing' in relation to this novel.

Writing

It is a commonplace (perhaps even a dreary one) of much contemporary criticism that writing, or its cognates, reading, interpretation, creation, is in self-referential ways about writing itself. Readers are most familiar with this through the endless numbers of novels about novelists writing novels. (*David Copperfield* (1849–50) was Dickens's foray into the autobiography of a writer.) Modern criticism, following modern art, has become acutely self-conscious. Whether as a protective carapace or as a means of establishing some rapport with over-educated readers, novelists feel that not to include some of the business of writing is not to write a novel at all. Indeed, it might now be that the definition of the serious modern novel is just that misplaced talent for self-consciousness; self-awareness becomes a writer's second skin. To put it schematically, and therefore more crudely than it really is, novels have a sort of interior literary essence as well as their social meanings. Just as the human body has its palpable and visible form, it also has its investigatable existence as anatomy or physiology, so in the same way, novels, even of this classic realist type, have a mimetic or representational purpose, but also a self-referential one. They tell us, in different ways, something about themselves as fictions, and about the informing consciousness of them as fictions.

Writers can, through this medium, inform us of what they think about writing, about language, about the relation of fiction to reality, even about the novel which is being written as we read it. Writers may express a confidence and defence of the fiction within in this way so as to offset malicious or doubtful readers. This may use the analogies of creation, or writing, of fictions, to express the doubts about the value of fiction. Since critics are themselves writers, they often catch on to these hints and guesses, and they can, in their zeal for the literary, mistake the small detail for the larger concern. Criticism's sharp focus easily can reduce to hazy background what actually goes on in novels, the action, the characters, the feelings evoked, the descriptions; often the first victim is the story or plot.

Yet, having said all this, and with due reservation, one does not have to make any very special sort of claim to see that *Hard Times* is concerned directly with reading and writing, with its own literariness, in other words. The novel is full of references to these activities, and not only because it begins in a schoolroom, the home of basic literacy. They can be emphasised in such a way that we can see how reading and by implication, writing, are larger cultural questions which relate directly to the themes of the novel, and are not *merely* exercises in a showy self-consciousness. There is too much going on in a nineteenth-century novel to reduce it merely to expressing embarrassment of the anxiety of writing, even when fiction itself is under discussion, but it is a sufficiently important part of the novel's meaning to warrant our attention.

Dickens always regarded himself as a professional writer, and he regarded that profession as an honourable one. But, as we have seen, some critics have thought *Hard Times* a poor defence of literature, of fiction against fact. If the fiction of the novel is to be equated with the circus and its improvised language, and freedom, then they are probably right. But I think that the reverse is true, and that Dickens makes a good case for literature, for fiction, and the language of fiction, by revealing (consciously or unconsciously is another matter) the doubt of undertaking the enterprise in the first place.

This produces a more realistic, if a less blithely confident case for fiction and fable in a scientifically-based society. The doubt is released through several means. Dickens is never cynical about writing, nor is he unduly sceptical about it. What, rather, he expresses is a sort of doubt that it will not have the confident power to stand up against his opponents. He does not doubt the novel form, but he recognises that novels must change. The judgement which Leavis reached was partly the right one; this is a 'serious' work of art. Where his criticism went awry is that his conclusion did not follow from his evidence. The creativity (a Leavis word) lies not only in the circus performers or in Sissy's angel of the house, but just as much in the creative manipulation of the monstrous characters, Bounderby, Sparsit, Gradgrind, even Bitzer in his own way. It lies just as much in the linguistic texture as in the broad symbol.

Language doubt

In one of his authorial indictments of the threat which the language of abstraction creates, Dickens says:

> So many hundred Hands in this Mill; so many hundred horse Steam Power. It is known, to the force of a single pound weight, what the engine will do; but, not all the calculators of the National Debt can tell me the capacity for good or evil, for love or hatred, for patriotism or discontent, for the decomposition of virtue into vice, or the reverse, at any single moment in the soul of one of these its quiet servants, with the composed faces and the regulated actions. There is no mystery in it; there is an unfathomable mystery in the meanest of them, for ever. Supposing we were to reserve our arithmetic for material objects, and to govern these awful unknown quantities by other means! [p. 108]

The general sense of this denunciation is clear. The language of statistical abstraction cannot measure human values, and should not be used to even try to. To attempt to dispel the mystery of the human soul is not only not desirable, it is not possible. Because it is not possible, the attempt is all the more malign.

What, though, is worth remarking on is the use of the verb 'govern'. To use such a word is to concede part of the case against which he is arguing: governance is necessary, he is admitting. It is a small, but telling example of Dickens's rhetoric of irony that he uses the language of his opponents – they are the people who would think of these qualities as 'awful, and unknown' (the sentiments and passions in other words), not Dickens. The excess of the irony is to show the powerlessness of the attack by agreeing to the perceptions of one's opponents in language. Now, whether Dickens really was confused about the feelings which cannot be accommodated within rigid systematisation or whether he believed what he seems to be saying is made unclear by this rhetoric. Govern is not the word one would normally think of for feelings, for human souls. We tend to think of words of expansion and liberation, not of constriction and regulation. But Dickens's overreaching language is to make part of the opponent's case, and thus his critique becomes not a clear condemnation of their heartlessness, soullessness, their economicism (seeing the word through the Benthamite calculus), but becomes symptomatic of the very heartlessness he is attacking, and he is thus committed to their language at the same time as he is exposing it for its misplaced application.

It is the doubleness of the ironic rhetoric which contains the doubt. A free language should not need to be tangled up with one's adversaries' language. In other words, one can see here how the irony is reactive and adversarial towards what exists as a formulation of an accepted order which Dickens partly undermines, but, and it is his concession, he is partly undermined by. That the unknown awful quantities should indeed be awful or unknown, or that they should be governable at all is to concede what the rest of the passage, and indeed, the whole thrust of the book is seeking to attack.

It is at the level of language that Dickens is curiously contradictory of the power of his satire. Can the mystery be preserved, is what he would like to ask: what he does ask is the less free question his opponents ask, how are we to regulate this ungovernable area of life? Elsewhere, he pleads that the province is best left to some measure of spontaneity and freedom. He calls for 'the cultivation of their sentiments and the affections', and cultivation is not government, but is in opposition to its authority. There he uses the growth and expansion metaphor, not the constrictive one, even if the terms he uses, 'sentiments', 'affections' may seem old-fashioned. This cultivation (ironically echoed in the novel's major divisions of 'Sowing, Reaping, Garnering') is to take place by the use of the methods which are opposed to those in use in Gradgrind's school system.

But the doubts which merge in the language of the satire, partly through authorial irony, partly through the hesitancies played with fictions (Mrs Sparsit's staircase), do not weaken Dickens's opposition in his broad purpose, but they rightly modify our views of what fictions can and cannot do. It was, after all, right that he should have had doubts.

This doubt can lead to two modes of attack. One is the highly-charged rhetorical denunciation (the language of the Bible, and its metaphors are always near the surface), of the narrator as in the passage above. Or, it can lead to a cool appraisal of the arguments which are needed against the economic bloodlessness of the *laissez-faire* economists, the 'hard fact' men. The second is not really the option for a dramatic satirist, but the first runs up against the danger of satirical irony which may undercut the other modes in the novel, in particular, the dramatic. Irony, particularly when used in the narrator's controlling demagogic voice, can become a sort of self-protective device, but one which, when examined, reveals the doubt and contradictions which it is seeking to allay. This is not to say that Dickens is not in control of what he is doing, so far as post-structuralism ever allows us to say that, but that the effect of what he is doing may also reveal, deep in his consciousness, the doubts of doing it in the first place.

And it is not difficult to argue that Dickens is unclear whether he is attacking abstraction, or something else. There is in this novel (and in his others too), a powerful anti-intellectual thrust in him, and, sometimes, his anti-intellectualism becomes hopelessly confused with his anti-utilitarianism. Admittedly, this might not be that difficult an error to make because utilitarianism itself seems to favour the pragmatic (hard-fisted chaps says Bounderby) against the theoretical, the action against the idea. But this is more apparent than real.

Fact and fiction

What is the reality of fact and fiction, the two key words of this novel? *Hard Times* relentlessly interrogates the meaning of these words, such that the novel becomes an extended essay on language, in particular, on how meanings cohere and are created by their users. Fact turns out not to be as Mrs Gradgrind and Bounderby pretend it is, and certainly not as simple as the answers to the question asked of Bitzer and Sissy. Take the famous opening paragraph:

> Now, what I want is, Facts. Teach these boys and girls nothing but Facts. Facts alone are wanted in life. Plant nothing else, and root out everything else. You can only form the minds of reasoning animals upon Facts; nothing else will ever be of any service to them. [p. 47]

Everyone recalls these chilling words in this grim schoolroom. And as the novel progresses, we see how fact is opposed to fancy, and how Gradgrind is magnetically attracted to the word. In that process fact ceases to be something simple in easily definable contexts, but takes on various meanings. Fact becomes whatever its users wish to invoke. Rather than the basis upon which knowledge may be founded, it becomes an inhibitor of thought and analysis. This paragraph is already showing some confusion. What, after all, is a fact? Is it something defined, an integer of knowledge with clear reference? The bleakness of learning nothing but fact is easily satirised (it is so improbable for one thing). But the middle sentence is more puzzling. There is a slight, but significant shift of meaning here. If you are to be a 'reasoning animal', one of the ends of education which is surely not ignoble, then reasoning must be based upon something. And the usual word for that knowledge is fact. Is Dickens therefore saying we should have no reasoning at all? Or is he saying something much subtler than this, as all the characters will reveal in the end, that reasoning and argument are also based upon feeling and desire?

Fact on the one hand is used to mean a conventionalised quasi-scientific discourse ('Quadruped. Gramnivorous. Forty teeth,' etc.), but it also is made to mean misuse of that discourse in a context for which it is inappropriate. This becomes much more explicit later on in the novel when fact is turned into fiction. But one wonders if the word 'fact' is being given too much meaning to bear. Sissy is thrown into confusion by the questioner, and is unable to offer the text definition. Bitzer does so effortlessly. Dickens thus makes the literary joke into a moral one. For the point of his famous horse definition is not that it is a fact, but that it is a body of knowledge in conventionalised form which is inappropriate for young children. Bitzer is a good pupil of inapposite knowledge. He learns to learn, whilst Sissy is revealed as ignorant. It is because she is uneducated that she can use only ungrammatical language. 'He belongs to the horse-riding, if you please sir', and she gains our sympathy as she faces Gradgrind's interrogation. 'Its father as calls me Sissy, sir' (a parody of the theatrical master of the house and servant-girl routine). But her plight is that she is blameless because she has yet to be educated.

The education theme is returned to in 'Sissy's Progress'. Now, several months later, Sissy has received some education. Whereas, in the first scene she was a totally innocent victim, now one is not too sure. Dickens makes Sissy almost perversely resistant to education. Here Sissy is telling Louisa in her own words about her progress (or lack of it) at school. As in a fairy tale, she is asked three questions, not one of which she can answer to the satisfaction of her school teacher.

When asked what is the first principle of this science (political economy) she replies. 'To do unto others as I would that they should do unto me.' [p. 95] When asked a question on the proportion of 25 in a million, she responds that 'it must be just as hard upon those who were starved, whether the others were a million, or a million million.' [p. 97]

And, when asked a question on the percentage of five hundred killed of a hundred thousand, she answers that the percentage is 'Nothing, Miss – to the relations and friends of the people who were killed.' [p. 98]

What are we meant to make of all this? Is it nothing more than Sissy's own confession that she is anxious to learn, wishes to honour her departed father but that, as far as education is concerned, she doesn't like it? Sissy is a pleasant, warm-hearted, circus girl, but education is not for her. If it were that alone, then nothing more need be said. But we are not meant, I think, to leave this dislike as simply one girl's simple inability to do arithmetic. The irrelevant answers suggest something more.

Sissy's responses are comic to an adult reader. As a feeling child (over-sentimentalised perhaps, but good-hearted nevertheless in a world in which such a quality is in drastically short supply), she mouths the human conditions which underlie the statistics. Like the strange Paul Dombey in *Dombey and Son* (1847–8) who asks his commercially successful father, 'What's money?', the child's innocence is used as an ironic device for a sort of lateral thinking. In a child we see such questioning as innocent, and in the eyes of her teacher as stupid. But to the adult reader, it is ironically comic because its humour lies in its subversion as it honestly denies the terms upon which the question is asked. Here, lateral thinking is almost like literal thinking, itself a mixture of the humorous and the inane so as to arrive at the serious. Behind the facts and figures are misery, pain, hunger, death, etc. This incident is designed to be typical of Dickens's intention to satirise a particular sort of mentality, an intention he sought to clarify when he wrote to C. Payne Knight:

> My satire is against those who see figures and averages and nothing else – the representatives of the wickedest and most enormous vice of the time, the men who through long years to come, will do more damage to the real useful truths of political economy than I could if I tried in my whole life. (*Knight*, 1873, pp. 187–8)

But, though he is careful to add the qualifier, 'and nothing else', what Sissy's pathetic attempts to achieve an elementary education represent is the relationship of language to reality.

It is difficult to believe that Dickens, in many ways a very worldly man (an author who led a life as a public figure), and one who knew all about fractions and proportions, if only in his dealing with his publishers!, can be endorsing the view that children should not be taught arithmetic. But let us look at the verbal framing of the mathematical questions. This is made into an attack on the dismal science of economics ('those who see figures and averages and nothing else') more than it is on the skill of manipulation of figures in arithmetic; it is not an invective against basic learning, but on the language of abstraction which makes us forget for what purposes language may be used, and how some usage may conceal human concern and deny human compassion. The identical point is made of Slackbridge's rhetorical address to the trades unionists. And, earlier in the novel, the same point was made concerning the definitions of the horse, and the appropriateness of having flowers decorating a wall; abstractions can mask truth, particularly horrible truths, and the disjunction that masking causes can produce humour and irony.

Now, clearly, Sissy's way of seeing the world and her teacher's way of seeing the world are basically at odds; if pushed to their logical conclusions they cannot be reconciled. Here the victory goes to the circumspect. Louisa, who does not love her father, but does what the education system demands of her, and the gentle Sissy, who does love hers, but who fails educationally (a neat little contrast). Our sympathies are with them, particularly as we have been exposed to 'fact' in the scenes describing Gradgrind's obsession and Bounderby's bullying. This conflict is played out throughout the novel. It is finally brought to a climax in the chapter 'Philosophical' which I shall deal with later.

And yet, there is something unsatisfactory in the two girls' opposition to their education. The point remains that no developed or indeed adult society can avoid the need for generalisation or abstraction as it applies to language. Is Dickens then merely a sort of philistine himself, an educational Luddite, against all modes of thinking which depend on generalisation and which subjugate the particular individual? This, of course, was the nub of Holloway's criticism, and it is an accusation often levelled against Dickens that in his created world, no thinking, because there is no abstraction, would be possible. Sissy's reaction, heart-warming and humorous as it is, may be very human, but it is also egocentric. It is anarchic too, as literal/lateral thinking often is. George Santayana, who is often invoked to prove that Dickens's characters are real (Santayana's famous remarks are cited by Leavis), nevertheless also said, but this is rarely quoted, that 'a community of eccentrics is impossible'. If Sissy were not typical, this would not matter. Unfortunately she is.

What can be said more comfortably is that what is faulty with the questions asked of Sissy is that they are irrelevant. She is receiving an education ('a sound practical education', Gradgrind informs her), which is wholly inappropriate for what she is going to do and be in this society. Sissy is not going to be a member of Parliament, nor a social commentator on economics, but the education handed down to her by Gradgrind, a political figure, eventually an MP, is at a level of generalisation which is largely irrelevant, as Dickens sees it, for her running her own life. It is an education from the 'top down', we would now say, and, like all top-down schemes, favours those at the top at the expense of those at the bottom, satisfies the former's preferences, privileges and ideas, but fails lamentably to take a true account of the people for whom the education is ostensibly created. This is an insightful, indeed sound, educational critique, of its sort. The education satire is not meant to be isolated in the novel, but is to be seen as how education will both give rise to and confirm the fact-society, and Gradgrind's and Bounderby's places within it.

Craig's observation that 'the linking of the classroom and mill turns out to be one of Dickens's most telling ways of composing his sense of English civilisation into a coherent, many-sided image' (*Craig*, p. 20) is sympathetic, but it may not actually stand up to what the novel does. The links are certainly made, but Sissy's inability to do arithmetic or Louisa's coldness may be determined by, but not as Dickens wants us to see, caused by, the Gradgrind education.

So if Dickens is not against basic learning, what exactly *is* he satirising? What, to return to Fielding's question, is his broad purpose? What he means by fact, then is not basic empirical knowledge, not fact at all. Nor, as it is opposed to fancy, is going to the circus, gratuitous laughter, fun, etc., but the other elaborated meaning in which fact, as it appears in the life of Gradgrind and Bounderby is a theoretical understanding carried almost to limitless excess. When all human activity is converted into a language code, a discourse here called facts and then pursued with an obsessive monomaniacal obsession, even though the experience in front of your eyes tells you differently, then you have no longer fact; what you have, is fiction. The ultimate concern is not with reality, but with the language expression of that reality. Once one has fabricated a discourse, everything can be made to fit.

This theoretical, supposedly fact-based, but actually excessive systemisation is what amounts to Dickens's focus of attack. The fact of school gives rise to the distorted fiction of life. Now this, in one sense, is a paradox for a writer to adopt. But it exists at the level of language analogies all the way through. The conflict of fact and fiction begins to appear less clear-cut the more one looks at how the words are used. One can call the fact-ridden systematisers the sociological imagination which has its own way of seeing the world and had its contemporary relevance in nineteenth-century society.

One can see how the situation arises when Dickens tells us of Gradgrind's school, 'It was his school, and he intended it to be a model. He intended every child in it to be a model – just as the young Gradgrinds were all models.' [p. 53] The dangerously rapid transition from an institution to a person is what gives the game away; they become like their geological specimens. They are reduced from the fully human, which means imperfect, irrational, desiring human beings. Mrs Gradgrind rebukes Louisa after she has admitted being at the circus. 'Go and besomethingological.' It is a nice but pointed confusion, Mrs Gradgrind sympathetically supporting her husband's fanatical educational system, but not understanding it. Her ignorance, on the other hand, shows Dickens's irony; 'doing' somethingological, is the very confusion which the system produces. Mrs Gradgrind cannot even separate the words. At least Gradgrind knows what he is doing; Mrs Gradgrind simply abets him because she thinks he is right.

What then appears to be happening is that 'fact' collapses into a sort of fiction. Language, once it takes over loses its referential solidity and becomes an irresponsible action and creation of its own. And this unstable, volatile condition of language is naturally one which concerns a creator of fictions. The highly schematised opposition of fact and fiction, particularly of fable, becomes unclear because fact and fiction become intertwined. Those who are the propounders of fact are fictionalisers. Both Bounderby and Gradgrind exemplify the fanatical commitment to the language of abstraction, and by so doing end up as analogies or metaphors for false creation.

Bounderby's 'fictions'

Bounderby, like Gradgrind, Mrs Sparsit, and Sleary is a strong character in the novel, not only in the sense of his domination of others by sadistic bullying (it is worth noting that such vicious treatment is meted out to his wife, his mother, his housekeeper, and, as we shall see below, to Mrs Gradgrind – all females who are in a subservient position to him), but in his creation and use of language. As he tells the unfortunate Mrs Gradgrind:

'Josiah Bounderby of Coketown learnt his letters from the out-sides of the shops, Mrs Gradgrind, and was first able to tell the time upon a dial-plate, from studying the steeple clock of St Giles's Church, London, under the direction of a drunken cripple, who was a convicted thief and an incorrigible vagrant. Tell Josiah Bounderby of Coketown, of your district schools and your model schools, and your training schools, and your whole kettle-of-fish of schools; and Josiah Bounderby of Coketown, tells you plainly, all right, all correct – he hadn't such advantages – but let us have hard-headed, solid-fisted people – the education that made him won't do for everybody, he knows well – such and such education was, however, and you may force him to swallow boiling fat, but you shall never force him to suppress the facts of his life.' [pp. 60–1]

Later on (Book 3, Chapter 5), we learn just the opposite. Mr
Bounderby has very carefully suppressed the facts of his life. His
mother makes clear to the assembly in his front room that 'he come
of humble parents, that he come of parents that loved him as dear as
the best could, and never thought it hardship on themselves to pinch
a bit that he might write and cypher beautiful, and I've his books at
home to show it!' [p. 280] But it suits Bounderby to dispense with
his real past and create, through his language, his fictional one
which supports his hard-headed philosophy. But more than this
Dickens indicates to us, Bounderby is a sign reader. His reading
education has been in his mind (but not in his actual experience),
reduced to learning about language by reading shop signs, a witty
synecdoche of the materialist mind. Once this has occurred, sign
reading takes over from an implied full reading.

When Bounderby reflects on who could possibly have stolen the
money from the bank the simplicity of his thinking becomes based
upon this abstracted reading. He immediately concludes, therefore,
that Stephen Blackpool is the thief. Simplified texts and reduced
reading make for simplified thinking. Since Stephen has complained
about working conditions, he must, therefore be a thief. Bounderby's
response is a literal one. '"But I am acquainted with these chaps,"
said Bounderby. "I can read 'em off like books."' The point is that
the proper reading of books would not allow for such a simple
reading. More pointedly, Bounderby himself is a figure with whom
the word 'fiction' is closely associated, but in a negative ironical
sense. When Stephen complains, Bounderby immediately translates
this into 'a dissatisfied Hand . . . a man that's fit for anything bad.'
This, says Dickens, is 'another of the popular fictions of Coketown,
which some pains had been taken to disseminate – and which some
people really believed.' [p. 211] Here, the word fiction is used
negatively, as if fiction itself is a bad thing to have in such a society,
which is a paradoxical thing for a writer to include in his text. Like
the use of the word 'govern', the meaning as used by its opponents
is allowed a certain strength in the process of making the opposite
case. Dickens is treading perilously close to the edge of self-criticism
when fiction is to be associated with those who create stories and
tales, but when those stories are false and malicious.

A small, but not insignificant moment which also casts its doubt
on the nature of these creative figures in the text, analogues for
creations and fictions, is a line which contains an awful pun, which
only comes to recognition if we see these characters as story-tellers.

Mrs Sparsit, we are told 'was a most wonderful woman for prowling about the house. How she got from storey to storey was a mystery beyond solution', where storey means not only level of house, but how she inhabits her own fictional world, creating staircases for Louisa to fall down, or imagining herself as a fairy dragon. Like Gradgrind (the ogre) or Bounderby, she is a debased story teller of dreadful fairy tales.

Dickens's positive synonym for fiction is fable, and this is given its fullest importance in the description of the institutional house of fables, which is the description of the local library, yet another comment on the place of fiction in people's lives:

> There was a library in Coketown, to which general access was easy. Mr Gradgrind greatly tormented his mind about what the people read in this library; a point whereon little rivers of tabular statements periodically flowed into the howling ocean of tabular statements, which no diver ever got to any depth in and came up sane. It was a disheartening circumstance, but a melancholy fact, that even these readers persisted in wondering. They wondered about human nature, human passions, human hopes and fears, the struggles, triumphs and defeats, the cares and joys and sorrows, the lives and deaths, of common men and women! They sometimes, after fifteen hours' work, sat down to read mere fables about men and women, more or less like themselves, and about children, more or less like their own. They took De Foe to their bosoms, instead of Euclid, and seemed to be on the whole more comforted by Goldsmith than by Cocker. Mr Gradgrind was for ever working, in print and out of print, at this eccentric sum, and he could never make out how it yielded this unaccountable product. [p. 90]

Dickens is quite clear why people will turn to fables, and not be satisfied with mere facts (statistics and blue books), or what Gradgrind sees as an unaccountable product. Mere fables ('mere' accented heavily with irony), are important sources of knowledge about human life, as well as the means of self-improvement and understanding. But, of course, they are fables, and in Bounderby's or Gradgrind's eyes 'the fictions of Coketown'. Defoe and Goldsmith are well chosen as they were both authors read by children, and Defoe would have been a useful allusion in that the originator of the prose novel himself chose humble citizens to write about. For the

Gradgrind who believes everything to be 'a case of simple arithmetic' [p. 48] such time wasting is literally incomprehensible.

Thus the conflict of fact and fiction turns out to be a conflict of different ways of reading, and of reading different things. Schematically, there are those who are the readers of the abstract, and those who are readers of the fable, but as the self-creating characters show, the distinction is not all that clear. All are varieties of reading and writing.

One of the interesting paradoxes is that the circus people are also 'sign-readers'. Mr Childers, like Bounderby, can read the signs; in the former case, both literally and metaphorically.

The Pegasus's Arms

The name of the public house was the Pegasus's Arms. The Pegasus's legs might have been more to the purpose; but underneath the winged horse upon the sign-board, the Pegasus's Arms was inscribed in Roman letters. Beneath that inscription again, in a flowing scroll, the painter had touched off the lines:

> Good malt makes good beer,
> Walk in, and they'll draw it here;
> Good wine makes good brandy,
> Give us a call, and you'll find it handy.

Framed and glazed upon the wall behind the dingy little bar, was another Pegasus – a theatrical one – with real gauze let in for his wings, golden stars stuck on all over him, and his ethereal harness made of red silk.

As it had grown too dusky without, to see the sign, and as it had not grown light enough within to see the picture, Mr Gradgrind and Mr Bounderby received no offence from these idealities. [p. 70]

What is important here is that this popular advertising jingle, and the mythical fabulous Pegasus are not shown as something naively positive, representing great art, if indeed art is the word to use at all, but, as the exposure of Master Kidderminster, a few paragraphs later, reveals, the circus is seen as a fake, if an authentic one. The touch is light with Childers and Kidderminster. The 'infant son' is in reality disclosed from the outset, as 'made up with curls, wreaths, wings, white bismuth, and carmine, this hopeful young person soared into so pleasing a Cupid ... but, in private, where his characteristics were a precocious cutaway coat and an extremely gruff voice, he became of the Turf, turfy.' [p. 72] Seeing the circus as a fable, as a fiction, is a way of understanding its true purpose.

Projected, this argument shows Dickens making a discrimination between fable and 'true' art, by showing that the false may contain good-heartedness and the true, because factual, may be, as is proved by the careers of Bounderby, Gradgrind and Sparsit, false. The 'idealists' are known to be fictions, and are not to be confused as standing in the place of fact. Language, as here, may contain a shabby reality; beneath the tinsel and gauze, and the make-up, lies something ordinary, but also something transforming. Master Kidderminster is not an infant son at all. The circus too is a fiction, and for these inhabitants of Coketown a necessary one, tawdry as it may be.

The attack on the theoreticians of language who deny the fake reality which may underlie it, is seen again in the metaphors which Dickens uses to show how such thought is created. In Mr Gradgrind's room, there is introduced the metaphor of science.

As if an astronomical observatory should be made without any windows, and the astronomer within should arrange the starry universe solely by pen, ink and paper, so Mr Gradgrind, in *his* Observatory (and there are many like it), had no need to cast an eye upon the teeming myriads of human beings around him, but could settle all their destinies on a slate, and wipe out all their tears with one dirty little bit of sponge. [pp. 131–2]

The windowless observatory is one equivalent to a closed mind. But Dickens contrasts the instruments of science and art and of language with the myriads who are to be represented by the agency of these instruments, and shifts the metaphor in mid-sentence from pen and ink to slate and sponge, thus harking back to schoolroom chalk and the ease with which human intractability is reducible by abstraction. And, indeed, childhood chalk and adult pen and ink are related because Louisa too can only think of others as less than human. 'She knew them in crowds passing to and from their nests, like ants or beetles. But she knew from her reading infinitely more of

the ways of toiling insects than of these toiling men and women.'
[p. 187] Louisa's natural history is almost unnatural.

Dickens is fond of using writing metaphors through the text. His
final one is an attempt to bring the whole novel together, when he
remarks that Sissy is:

> trying hard to know her humbler fellow-creatures, and to beautify
> their lives of machinery and reality with those imaginative graces
> and delights, without which the heart of infancy will wither up,
> the sturdiest physical manhood will be morally stark death, and
> the plainest national prosperity figures can show, will be the
> Writing on the Wall. [p. 313]

The capitalised symbol, originally a phrase for the literal passing
of the death sentence is meant to make the equivalence that bad art
and bad lives, or at least reduced texts (signs), lead to spiritual
vacuity. The language of abstraction is a kind of death sentence, a
metaphor which harks back to the book's opening, where Chapter 2
is entitled 'Murdering the Innocents'.

Language and the self

William Oddie's study of *Hard Times* (1973), which traced the
influence of Carlyle's tormented anti-materialism on Dickens con-
cluded that the novel was an attack on 'perverted rationalism'. But
this can be further refined, as the numerous writing and reading
metaphors suggest, as a specific attack on the perversions of an
abstract and dehumanised discourse. It is not merely ideas which
are under attack, but the ways in which those ideas come about and
are disseminated, the ways in which discourse is created by selves
and selves create discourse. The link of schoolroom and industry is
meant as a dire warning. If children are given only one language,
then naturally, they will use it. Unfortunately, when adults, they
will also use it naturally (or unthinkingly) which can be even more
insidious. What is less clear, though, is whether Dickens believes, to
put it abstractly, that psychology precedes discourse, or discourse
precedes psychology. Do people act and talk as they do because
there is a socially sanctioned language which allows them to act in
their outrageously egocentric ways? Or does the dehumanised discourse, the reduced formulae, the language of facts and figures make

them what they are? Would another discourse produce different sorts of people, with more attractive behaviour? Clearly, the answer partly depends on whether we think Dickens was an optimist or a pessimist. Usually, it is affirmed that Dickens was the former. But the novel entertains both views.

If *Hard Times* is taken as saying that an impoverished educational system produces blighted lives, then there is the implicit assumption that amelioration is possible through more sensitive and imaginative schooling. An improved schooling system will produce a better, more humane society, with no Gradgrinds or Bounderbys. Much as Dickens the public reformer might have wanted to believe this, the book provides counter-evidence, both positively and negatively, that education is ultimately irrelevant to what people are. Sissy, after all, perhaps over-emphatically, fails entirely, yet is a warm, affectionate and socially desirable person. Education does not change her fundamental character at all. Louisa, who seems to have a character created entirely by the system, is its worst victim. A good education may do good, but a bad one certainly does harm. But if education cannot necessarily do good, then this implies that people are what they are in some fundamental irreducible sense, and education can be useful or not useful to them. *Hard Times* cannot be claimed to be optimistic if it does not propose that good must come of good education.

A much more worrying reflection on this question of the self and the language it may employ is provided by the character of Harthouse. He is a striking instance of the disparity between language and reality when he half-proudly proclaims:

The result of the varieties of boredom I have undergone, is a conviction (unless conviction is too industrious a word for the lazy sentiment I entertain on the subject), that any set of ideas will do just as much good as any other set, and just as much harm as any other set. [p. 162]

This 'vicious assumption of honesty in dishonesty', as Dickens puts it, he means us to see as more dangerous than the hypocrisy of Bounderby. It anticipates the spiritual death which will afflict Louisa later on. 'Everything being hollow and worthless, she had missed nothing and sacrificed nothing.' [p. 195] The connection is the clear one that if everything is of equal value, then nothing means anything. We can see here that behind the attack on systematisation or needless abstraction lies something more profound, as both Harthouse and in a different but far from worrying way Bitzer represent, which Gradgrind, a dupe of his own system, and Bounderby, merely a vicious opportunist if a temporarily successful one within it, do not. In a word, nihilism.

But there is also a lingering doubt which creative writers are familiar with, which is that Harthouse's cynicism contains also a truth. It is not a pleasant truth, nor is it a reassuring one, especially to those critics who would describe Dickens as a simple-minded moralist. It is that language, or writing, can be something not absolute but relative. Its users, like Harthouse, need not believe in what the words mean. They need not believe in their use of language, which is the interpretation of reality and hence any behaviour is justified ('just as much good', 'just as much harm'). Dickens makes the point through his narrator's comment that language without belief is 'deadly', and 'common'. The analogue for Dickens the novelist is that fiction can go seriously wrong, and do serious moral harm, if not informed by a sustained moral interest. Dickens was not a paid-up sceptical philosopher, but the novel allows doubt to enter. The novel entertains those doubts, but it has to overcome them. Partly, this is because the self-creating, self-dramatising fictions of Bounderby and Sparsit are revealed as fictions, and dangerous ones, and ultimately because with the author's manipulation, they are heartless but defeatable ones. Partly, though, it is because the system of which they are embodiments is shown to be so callous.

But what confirms the novel as a serious discussion of the relation between language and selfishness is brilliantly dramatised in the chapter entitled 'Philosophical' which is the resolution of the plot, if not the novel. It is here we can see at its best Dickens's skill as a dramatic writer for he gives the full dramatic weight to the scene in such a realised way that Bitzer is not merely a theatrical figure, but one who can, albeit, only in a utilitarian way, think and argue.

Up to this point Bitzer has been a shadowy figure who appears intermittently, in contrast to Sissy at school, in contrast to Tom in the bank. He appears as a curiously passive figure, cautious, sly, unimaginative, his colourlessness is his most telling feature. But what little we are told about him begins to make up the composite picture which this final scene will complete. He is deliberately underplayed. 'Bitzer' as a name suggests a composite sum of fragments, a person of 'bits'. His identity seems created out of the residue of other people's ideas. Yet, at the same time, he is the 'extremely clear headed, cautious, prudent young man, who was safe to rise in the world', who puts his mother in the workhouse but has doubts about allowing her even as much as half a pound of tea per year ('all gifts have an inevitable tendency to pauperize the recipient'), and who does not wish to marry because it is economically pointless. Bitzer is not humorously portrayed, and this is one of the more perplexing aspects of him. He is conformist, uncritical and far more dangerous than the shallow Harthouse. He is a deadly serious figure, and Dickens accords him a certain frosty respect whilst he condemns him with bitter irony. He is not a figure cosily dismissable like other figures.

Self-interest

It is important to consider the scene depicted in 'Philosophical' for the arguments it contains. Tom ('the deplorable object'), has been apprehended just as he is about to escape with the help of the circus people by Bitzer's coming on the scene. Mr Gradgrind pleads for his son, and Bitzer retorts rationally to this appeal. As readers we are put in the position to judge the case on both sides. An apologetic, and a humbled, reformed father who has taught his creed of self-interest to his most dedicated pupil, and who is not reformed by experience, is appealed to.

The conflict of ideas is parallel to that in which the ignorant Sissy offers her innocent response to Mr M'Choakumchild's interrogation. 'What is the first principle of this science?', 'To do unto others as I would that they should do unto me.' [p. 95] Rightly, Dickens calls this absurd. Indeed it is. Sissy sounds like some fluttery bishop answering a question about nuclear power. Bitzer responds in the way he has been so well schooled. What must be made clear is that he is being asked to break the law. He is being asked to allow a felon to escape, or at least to be an accessory in this robbery. He refuses to do this because as he makes clear to his former teacher, it is not in his best self-interest. 'But I am sure you know that the whole social system is a question of self-interest. What you must always appeal to, is a person's self-interest.' [p. 303] The words return to taunt Gradgrind.

Despite the fact that Gradgrind will make good the money taken from the bank, Bitzer realises he will be better off telling the truth than abetting the crime. He does not make his decision on moral grounds of someone else's choosing, but on the pragmatic grounds of what is best, financially, for himself, and what also will not contradict his own brand of pragmatic morality. He is strangely not corruptible here, and point for point he defeats Gradgrind. From Bitzer's point of view, his response is to defend his position. Why ruin your career for the sake of someone else's child and someone else's mistakes of which you have been the beneficiary? Why indeed? Bitzer's is a hard-headed morality, and it is based upon a shrewd calculation. The money which would buy his silence (he has no thoughts of revenge, and wonders why Gradgrind should bring in feelings at all) cannot be as great as that for being honest, and an unusual irony, but in this instance, true.

Here we have not only Bitzer's self-interest, but competing self-interests, and because Bitzer has the system and all the law on his side, he has the better argument. What, after all, *would* be the alternative for Bitzer? Bitzer should break the law, impair his own career by not taking advantage of the vacancy Tom's capture will create, lose money, all for the sake of a pretended sentimental attachment which Gradgrind never pretended to when he was teaching Bitzer, as his own words make clear?:

> 'Bitzer', said Mr Gradgrind, stretching out his hands as though he would have said, See how miserable I am! 'Bitzer, I have but one chance left to soften you. You were many years at my school. If, in remembrance of the pains bestowed upon you there – you can persuade yourself in any degree to disregard your present interest and release my son, I entreat and pray you to give him the benefit of that remembrance.'
>
> 'I really wonder, sir,' rejoined the old pupil in an argumentative manner, 'to find you taking a position so untenable. My schooling was paid for; it was a bargain; and when I came away the bargain ended.' [p. 304]

But this is a near pathetic afterthought on Gradgrind's part; it was never part of the original educational scheme. Nor is the law which Bitzer is upholding a bad one. Stealing money from a bank (even if the banker himself is wholly vicious) is not something which Dickens would have advocated. And yet, to criticise Bitzer would be in part to endorse the crime. Bitzer's response is uncharitable, unfeeling, selfish, but it is forensically correct. After all, Bitzer is not

Bounderby, he is not a rich capitalist manufacturer, but an aspiring employee, and he looks to the future of his bourgeois self-interest. Bitzer is not a hypocrite, that cosy, if shocking figure, for the typical nineteenth-century novel reader. Indeed, his ruthless rationalism exposes the hypocrisy which underlines Gradgrind's appeal. His personal profit can come about on the basis of others' personal weaknesses, and it is a savage law, says Dickens, that allows one to capitalise on it.

Unlike, Sissy, Bitzer is a realist. For him, all human relations are but money relations. Yet Dickens gives Bitzer a double advantage in this debate. He will not only be upholding the law, he will be gaining personal advantage from so doing. One can at this point argue that Dickens's satire, if it is to mean anything, must finally be against an inhumane system which produces this moral dilemma rather than individual behaviour within it. Bitzer's choice is of course cleverly selective. He chooses the arguments for the circumstances. In this case, they fit perfectly. The irony for Dickens is that the social arrangements, the ideology and the personal desires, all coincide to make a perfect fit. One has to admit that Bitzer gets the best of it.

The inverted parable

What is opposed to Bitzer's rational common sense is nothing less than Christian charity or biblical morality, as indeed it has been implicitly through the novel. The biblical language has not been chosen gratuitously. It is almost certain that the nineteenth-century reader would have been consciously aware, possibly more than the modern one, that one of the abiding lessons of Christianity was the parable of the Good Samaritan. (*Luke*, 29–37) This lesson of charity and compassion is specifically alluded to as something beyond Gradgrind's comprehension. 'He sat writing in the room with the deadly-statistical clock, proving something no doubt – probably, in the main, that the Good Samaritan was a Bad Economist.' [p. 238] This witty aphorism is expanded into a whole dramatic confrontation in 'Philosophical'. Bitzer's refusal of Gradgrind's appeal is an ironic reversal of the charitable and compassionate message which the parable holds, but it is one which is finally delivered by the merciful, if rather devious help of Sleary in helping Tom escape. The anarchic bohemian, frequently tipsy circus folk, are the Good Samaritans. As far as a fable goes this does not present any problems, but as a strong argument of a counterforce to Bitzer's argument of self-interest, it makes Dickens's implied positive a weak and naive one.

The Good Samaritan parable invites all too easily the cynical rejection which Bitzer willingly makes. It is not that the lesson of the Good Samaritan is not a good one, nor that Faith, Hope and Charity are not noble ideals. It is, rather, that this stark contrast between spiritual exaltation and materialist selfishness, has difficulty making sense in a realistic novel. Putting up Christian spiritual idealism against the world of legislated and scientific society makes for a useful protest, but it offers nothing in the way out of the problem. The Good Samaritan parable in the society of *Hard Times* is shown up as what it is, the simplest, yet most difficult and absurd of Christian messages. Despite Dickens's loosely held non-conformist religious views, he uses the parable here in a positive way. Yet, as with Sissy's response to her school teacher, the spiritual and the material cannot be reconciled. In practice, no doubt, and this was as true of Dickens's society (as it was of all his nineteenth-century critics) living by the precepts of compassion and by dedicated self-interest, afforded many people no problem. They lived with the contradiction, as they lived with any other contradiction. But in theory, where logic pushes the paradox for what it is, as here, then the paradox becomes an absurdity.

If self-interest is paramount, as Bitzer argues, then love for a stranger, unless it fits in with that self-interest, simply makes no sense at all. (The most devastating account of love for a stranger where self-interest is not involved, can be found in Freud's *Civilisation and Its Discontents* (1930) in which a materialist thinker ruthlessly exposes the ideal notion of loving one's neighbour as oneself or loving thine enemies as nonsensical and absurd. Freud's views to some may appear cynical, and to a believer in the Gospels, sacrilegious, but in his rational account he can find no reason, unless self-interest *is* the motivation, why anyone should act in this way and still claim to act rationally.

In a society committed to materialist greed founded upon self-interest, the lesson of the Good Samaritan may be an interesting spiritual idea, but, in *Hard Times*, it seems to be made into an idea which only those on the edges of decent, bourgeois society, such as the circus entertainers, can adopt and use. It has literally 'no meaning' for the other inhabitants of Coketown. For them, as for Freud, it is incomprehensible. When Mrs Gradgrind is dying, she concedes that Louisa learnt 'ologies of all kinds, from morning to night.' [p. 225] But when she tries to write that 'something – not an Ology at all – that your father has missed, or forgotten', all she can produce is little figures of no-meaning. The metaphor of gibberish, meaningless marks upon a paper (a writing metaphor) is the overwhelming defeat which the novel shows the blighted figures of the Gradgrind family suffering. It is left to the holy fools of the circus to produce the lesson of the Gospel.

One conventional and proper response would be to say that Bitzer, Tom and Louisa are characters without love, both in the human, sexual sense, and in the sense of Christian providence. Love is also part of the Christian message which the book offers, if only by its haunting absence. But Dickens's attack on Bitzer's selfishness (and Tom too is a study in self-interest), shows how they are caught up in capitalist society's inscription of materialism.

What is so remarkable about Bitzer, 'the rising young man', is that he can so coolly articulate the devastating basis of the materialist society in a way which, unlike Gradgrind and Bounderby, shows no rhetorical gesture of exaggeration. Dickens satirises Bounderby and Gradgrind, but Bitzer is a cool reasoner. When he makes his only long speech, he does not bluster, nor does he need to embroider his language.

Yet there is, perhaps, only one serious counterforce to Bitzer's selfishness, it seems to me, and that is Dickens's perception that the only check on unbridled individualism (one which Bitzer deliberately rejects with his refusal to be married and to have to keep a family) is parenthood. Here individual desire is abated. Gradgrind is used as an example of a man who fails, at first, to make the transition to parenthood. His methods of education which made him a successful hardware manufacturer are the very methods which bring about his downfall as a parent. When Tom is seen, finally, as a 'pathetic object', this is meant as a burning degradation to a middle-class parent, but Gradgrind is redeemed. Only Sissy has children in the novel's projected future.

Bitzer is used, then, not only to present the clearest case for self-interest, but also, finally, to bring the satire's concerns into a unity of interconnection. If we consider *Hard Times* like any other Dickens novel we could see it as a morality play on a single vice. And that vice would be selfishness. In such a play, altruism and love would be combated (Sissy, a reformed Gradgrind) against self-interest (Bounderby and Bitzer). But the novel is not as simple, despite its seeming schematic structure, as this would imply. There are different sorts of selfishness. Gradgrind is obsessed with his fact education, but he is unlike his son, 'always looking after No. 1'. Even in his unredeemed state, he is gentle to Sissy, and feels no contempt towards her. But the continual concern with writing, and writing's metaphors, points to something further than this old-fashioned morality. It is the connection between language and selfishness. Whereas the relationship for Louisa is that between discourse and despair, for Bitzer it is confidence and the 'philosophical'.

More interestingly, what Dickens's text reveals is that there is a profound, possibly deeply worrying relationship between language (or creation), and selfishness. Dickens would, no doubt, like to have us believe the opposite, and the act of writing a novel is a wholly generous and giving one. 'People must be amused', as Sleary says; children must have their fairy tales, the people their fables. But the end result of the novel is to entertain the strongest possible doubts about the efficacy of language and discourse. There are good languages and bad languages, good fictions and bad fictions. There can be the oppressiveness of strong creators. Bounderby shows all too clearly what can happen if the reality of other people is ignored. He is then free to imagine the most bizarre fictions about others, whilst condemning their views of themselves as fictions.

Bounderby and Gradgrind, eventually, are humbled, but Bitzer remains at the end of the novel as a created being who is not subject to failure, but success (of a sort). Bitzer is the monster created out of a theory. He is created out of a materialist discourse and he appears rational, sane, limited, but with a degree of realism, all the more frightening because he is so realistic. Dickens can, and indeed, does control his other creations, much as they try to create themselves. But Bitzer's 'tabula rasa passiveness' is not the work of some disciplinable puppet, but of a human being who fulfils the rational purpose of his creator. Bitzer is the end result of the perfected system of not only materialism, but of the abstractions of discourse which underlie it. In a novel without a hero, he becomes the only victor.

Epilogue

It is always foolhardy to invoke contemporary social and political concerns to describe works of literature which belong to older and different times. *Hard Times*, as I indicated in the Survey, is a mid-

Victorian novel. But, as was also argued in the Introduction, such pressing interests will emerge whether we like it or not, because literary criticism is inexorably bound upon the rack of its own time. Those aspects of the novel I have chosen to highlight are not only a reflection of the critic, but of the intellectual climate in which she/he writes.

Hard Times, if not the most diverting of Dickens's novels, is, nevertheless, perhaps because of its very abstraction which makes it the least diverting, one which has a certain relevance to recent history. It remains a political novel. This is not because it deals with political parties or a defunct parliamentary system (which rate only passing references in the book), but in the more generalised sense of what we recognise are ultimately political issues, of language, ideology and morality. One thing it shows very clearly, is how capitalism harnesses self-interest for its successes, and then how easily the appeal to self-interest can be made. Everyone knows about themselves; they do not know of others, nor do they live with others, or, even have to see them.

Bounderby is permitted the most outrageous statements about those who, like Stephen Blackpool, live a different life. Money allows him, as it does Bitzer, to get rid of other people, to buy their way out. The second thing which we are familiar with is that aspect of materialism which is not mere self-interest (dressed up as pious morality or not), but which is the frenzied obsession with the accounting for everything. 'What you couldn't state in facts and figures . . .'. The humble message of Sleary's Good Samaritan, which is an extension of the Christian principle that it is better to give than to receive is now strongly at variance with, and almost completely undermined by, the ethic of ambitious and materialist self-interest. Mrs Sparsit, when she offers Bitzer his lamb chop, walnut sauce and ale, nevertheless, declines to join him. 'She considered lunch a weakness', something we now expect of those, as Bounderby calls them 'Who know the value of time.' Food, given unconditionally, is a traditional gift of hospitality and generosity, but in Mrs Sparsit's mind, nothing is for nothing. As with the imaginary flowers in the schoolroom, traditional symbols for kindness are turned into symbols of something for something. Natural beneficence is made into something unthinkable.

Britain has, in the decade of the 1980s, witnessed a re-phrasing of the utilitarian ideology of self-interest and accountability. Indeed, it has had a government which has publicly proclaimed its wishes to return to 'Victorian values'. It has generated its own language, its mottoes and proverbs, and its own abstract discourse. One can only imagine what Dickens would have made of such phrases as 'the bottom line', 'there is no such thing as society' or 'consumer choice' or any of the other formulations which have resonated in the public discourse. It is unlikely he would have interrogated them any less fearlessly than he does the catch phrases in *Hard Times*.

And parallels can be easily drawn. The establishment of schools which are to be closely tied to industry and technology, the City Technology schools, and to be, in part, paid for by them, seems like a re-run of Gradgrind's mill. Bitzer's anxiety that allowing his mother a half a pound of tea a year in the workhouse is dangerous because 'gifts pauperise the recipient' is an idea which comes easily to those who bemoan 'the dependency culture'. Far-fetched as it may seem, that identical sentiment, and in virtually the same words, was declared by a politician in the House of Commons during the writing of this book.

But Dickens's satire is more than the indictment of greed and materialism. It is the connection between self-interest and the language which buttresses it, that is his underlying concern. Bitzer's everything is self-interest, and this has now been augmented by the unashamed 'greed is good', or the self-regarding 'me generation'.

When Leavis condemned the colourless boy as the triumph of the system, like Dickens, he used 'triumph' ironically. Now one cannot be too sure if Bitzer is not, in effect, the perfect model for the aspiring career-minded. In the 1980s slang, Bitzer, the rising young man, is an embryo 'yuppie'. He is not a grammar school child who, through scholarships has worked his way through the education system, a model for Britain for the past forty years; nor is he a product, as we may assume the languid Harthouse is, of those 'festering centres of snobbery', as Orwell called them, the public schools. He is a product of the school with the closest possible links with commerce and industry. Will the City Technology experiment aim to produce Bitzers?

Certainly, the uncompassionate, unyielding, rational, self-interested Bitzer would seem a model for which the recent government has craved. He is the supreme example of the enterprise culture. It is a huge irony that this monstrous child, the product of a theory and of commerce, should embody all the values which are so approved of by the materialistic politicians of our times. No doubt he would know a good bottom line if he saw one, quite unlike those anarchic folk in the leisure industry who spend their time in disastrous clowning, failed businessmen, in other words. Readers may care to draw their own comparisons, for there are several. However, it would be misleading to draw them in such a way as to suggest that our society is not also in many ways different from Dickens's. Not only is the circus no longer so important a form of entertainment, but organised religion is much less potent an influence, which is why the Christian morality seems so weak a counterforce to self-interest. Moreover, Dickens was not soft-headed, compassionate as he was, about technology, or industrial change and progress. He loved machinery, visited factories to research his journalism, and unlike many of his critics and contemporaries, welcomed the changes science brought. His was not a romantic Luddite intellect like Blake's.

What he did offer, with all its faults, was a broad-purposed, generous, humane critique of a society obsessed by ideology. He offered no practical solutions to its problems. This was not a novelist's task. He thought, perhaps wrongly, that it should have been and that perhaps novels can do more. But poets and novelists are not the unacknowledged legislators of the world, nor should they be. This is too worrying a fantasy. Dickens provided a critique which will inform our feelings and thoughts about abstract issues; it will dramatise and rehumanise the abstract. It may be a limited role, but it is a useful and vital one. Certainly, it is a necessary one in a free society which needs to remain alert to relinquishing everything to the materialist theorising abstractions of language. Dickens, as the novel's dedicatory epigraph announced, followed Carlyle and transcribed the 'Signs of the Times' by refusing to accept that everything must end up as the 'Times of the sign'. His major insight was that selfishness and the language of public discourse are deeply connected, but that his own society refused to see it. We perhaps see it too much, and do too little about it. And, finally, he thought that people must be 'amused'. Entertainment is necessary too, otherwise society becomes a dull and merciless place.

Selected Bibliography

The following is a selection of books and articles which I have found useful for the critical debate surrounding *Hard Times*. Also included are one or two less specific references which will allow for further exploration of the issues raised.

Several of the critical comments referred to in the Appraisal are conveniently gathered together in two collections:

George Ford and Sylvere Monod (eds), *Hard Times*, Norton Edition (New York, 1966). Essays by Hirsch, Martineau, Shaw.

Phillip Collins, *Dickens: the Critical Heritage* (London, 1971). Essays by Stephen, Ruskin, Whipple.

Richard D. Altick, *Victorian People and Ideas* (London, 1973).

F. G. Atkinson, '*Hard Times*: Motifs and Meanings', *Use of English*, vol. 14, 1963, pp. 165–9.

John Butt and Kathleen Tillotson, *Dickens at Work* (London, 1968).

R. C. Churchill, *A Bibliography of Dickensian Criticism 1836–1975* (New York and London, 1975).

Phillip Collins, *Dickens and Education* (London, 1963).

Steven Connor, *Charles Dickens* (Oxford, 1985).

R. J. Cruikshank, *Charles Dickens and Early Victorian England* (London, 1949).

Daniel P. Deneau, 'The Brother-Sister Relationship in Hard Times' in *The Dickensian*, vol. 60, 1964, pp. 173–7.

Monroe Engel, *The Maturity of Dickens* (London, 1959).

K. J. Fielding, *Charles Dickens: A Critical Introduction* (London, 1958 and 1965).

K. J. Fielding, 'Hard Times for the Present', *The Dickensian*, vol. 63, 1967, pp. 149–52.

John Forster (ed.), *The Life of Charles Dickens*, J. W. T. Ley (London, 1927).

Roger Fowler, 'Polyphony and Problematic in Hard Times' in *The Changing World of Dickens (ed.)* Robert Giddings (New York and London, 1983), pp. 91–108.

Sigmund Freud, *Civilization and Its Discontents*, Penguin Freud Library, vol. 12 (Harmondsworth, 1985).

John Gibson, 'Hard Times a Further Note', in *Dickens Studies*, vol. 1, 1965, pp. 90–101.

David M. Hirsch, '*Hard Times* and Dr. Leavis', *Criticism*, vol. VI (Winter, 1964), pp. 1–16.

John Holloway, 'Hard Times: A History and a Criticism', in *Dickens and the Twentieth Century* (eds) John Gross and Gabriel Pearson (London, 1962).

Edgar Johnson, *Charles Dickens: His Tragedy and Triumph* (Harmondsworth, revised edition, 1986).

Arnold Kettle, 'Dickens and the Popular Tradition' in David Craig (ed.) *Marxists on Literature* (Harmondsworth, 1975), pp. 214–44.

Charles Payne Knight, *Passages of a Working Life*, vol. III (1873), pp. 187–8.

F. R. Leavis, *The Great Tradition* (London, 1948).

Lawrence Lerner, 'An Essay on Dombey and Son' in *The Victorians* (London, 1978).

David Lodge, 'The Rhetoric of Hard Times', in *The Language of Fiction* (London, 1966), pp. 144–63.

Robert E. Longy, 'The Romance as Radical Literature', *Dickens Studies Annual*, vol. 2 (New York, 1980).

William Oddie, *Dickens and Carlyle: the Question of Influence* (London 1973).

George Orwell, 'Charles Dickens' in *Collected Essays and Journalism and Letters*, vol. 1 (Harmondsworth, 1970), pp. 454–504.

John Ruskin, 'A Note on Hard Times', *Cornhill Magazine*, vol. 2 (London, 1860).

Geoffrey Johnson Sadok, 'Dickens and Dr. Leavis. A critical Commentary on Hard Times', in *Dickens Studies Annual*, vol. 2 (New York, 1980), pp. 208–16.

George Bernard Shaw, Introduction to *Hard Times* (London, 1912).

James Fitzjames Stephen, 'Mr. Dickens as a Politician', *Saturday Review*, 3, January, 1857, iii, pp. 8–9.

René Wellek, *The Attack on Literature and Other Essays* (Sussex, 1982).

Edwin P. Whipple, *Atlantic Monthly*, March, 1877, xxxix, pp. 353–
   8.
Raymond Williams, *Culture and Society* (London, 1958).
Edmund Wilson, 'Dickens: The Two Scrooges', in *The Wound and
   the Bow* (London, 1961), pp. 1–93.
Warrington Winters, 'Dickens's *Hard Times*: the Lost Childhood', in
   Dickens Studies Annual, vol. 2 (New York, 1980), pp. 217–36.

Index